GRAMMAR FOR WRITING 2
AN EDITING GUIDE TO WRITING

Joyce S. Cain

ALWAYS LEARNING

PEARSON

Grammar for Writing 2: An Editing Guide to Writing

Pearson ELT, 10 Bank Street, White Plains, NY 10606

Staff credits: The people who made up the **Grammar for Writing 2** team, representing editorial, production, design, and manufacturing are: Pietro Alongi, Rhea Banker, Christine Edmonds, Nancy Flaggman, Jaime Lieber, Amy McCormick, Massimo Rubini, Paula Van Ells, and Marian Wassner.

Cover design: Barbara Perez
Text design: Barbara Perez
Text composition: ElectraGraphics, Inc.
Text font: ITC Stone Serif
Cover photo: John Elk/Getty Images

Library of Congress Cataloging-in-Publication Data
Cain, Joyce S.
  [Eye on editing]
Grammar for writing 1 : an editing guide to writing / Joyce S. Cain.
— 2nd ed.
      p. cm.
  Previously pub.: Eye on editing, 2001.
  Includes bibliographical references.
   ISBN 0-13-208898-3 — ISBN 0-13-208899-1 — ISBN 0-13-208900-9 1.
English language—Textbooks for foreign speakers. 2. English language—
Grammar—Problems, exercises, etc. 3. English language—Rhetoric—
Problems, exercises, etc. 4. Report writing—Problems, exercises, etc.
5. Editing—Problems, exercises, etc. I. Title. II. Title: Grammar
for writing one.
  PE1128.C25 2012
  808'.02—dc22

                                                2011008774

ISBN-10: 0-13-208899-1
ISBN-13: 978-0-13-208899-2

PEARSON LONGMAN ON THE **WEB**

Pearsonlongman.com offers online resources for teachers and students. Access our Companion Websites, our online catalog, and our local offices around the world.

Visit us at **pearsonlongman.com**.

Printed in the United States of America

7 17

Contents

To the Teacher

Grammar for Writing 2: An Editing Guide to Writing emphasizes the importance of the editing stage in the writing process. It is designed to meet the needs of ESL and developmental writers who have developed a high-intermediate level of fluency yet are unable to detect and correct grammatical errors in their writing. The concise grammatical explanations based on the most frequently occurring grammar errors of ESL students and the variety of editing exercises will help students begin to master the process of editing their own written work. *Grammar for Writing 2: An Editing Guide to Writing* can stand on its own or serve as a supplement to reading, writing, and grammar classes. It is also a useful reference guide for students.

The main goal of *Grammar for Writing 2: An Editing Guide to Writing* is to develop students' ability to detect errors in their own writing and provide them with the tools to make necessary corrections. It aids students in the production of accurate, meaningful, and appropriate language. To this end, the grammar explanations and rules focus on those errors that are most prevalent in the writing of students at the high-intermediate level, although the book is an appropriate review for students at the advanced level of writing proficiency as well.

Grammar for Writing 2: An Editing Guide to Writing is not intended to be a comprehensive grammar book. Grammar topics are based on an analysis of student writing errors. Because it focuses on specific problem areas, a cross-reference to three grammar books, *Fundamentals of English Grammar, Fourth Edition, Understanding and Using English Grammar, Fourth Edition,* and *Focus on Grammar 4, Fourth Edition,* has been provided to assist those who would like further grammatical explanations.

New to this Edition

A number of changes have been made in the second edition of *Grammar for Writing 2: An Editing Guide to Writing* based on feedback from teachers who use the book and from my own experiences using the book with students at both the university and community college levels.

- Three new chapters have been added: Word Forms, Verb Forms, and Prepositions. These new chapters replace the Noun Clauses and Word Order chapters, which have been moved to *Grammar for Writing 3: An Editing Guide to Writing.*

- Some effort was made to modify the language and sentence complexity in this edition. This change allows community college students greater comprehension of the concepts and content in each chapter while still addressing the grammar and writing concepts needed by university writers. While the vocabulary has been modified, it is based on the Academic Word List, developed in 2000 by Averil Coxhead from written vocabulary used in the fields of liberal arts, commerce, law, and science. Appendix 11 contains a list of vocabulary used in each chapter that comes from the Academic Word List.

- The Grammar Focus section has been moved to the beginning of each chapter to trigger student knowledge of the chapter's grammar point before the Pretest is presented.

- Following the Pretest, a short paragraph that contains multiple examples of the chapter's grammar concept gives students a contextualized presentation of this concept. This paragraph has students tap into their passive awareness of the grammar concept, giving them another opportunity to familiarize themselves with the concept before they are required to produce it actively.

- The Writing Topics section has been expanded to include a model student paragraph based on one of the writing topics that students are asked to write on. Students are instructed to notice the organization of the paragraph in addition to content that might help them as they begin to write their own paragraphs.

Although accurate editing remains the focus of *Grammar for Writing 2: An Editing Guide to Writing*, a greater emphasis is placed on writing in the second edition. Throughout the series, students work toward becoming independent writers who can plan, write, revise, and edit their work without relying on outside help.

Format and Content

Grammar for Writing 2: An Editing Guide to Writing is composed of twelve chapters. Eleven chapters focus on areas of grammar that are particularly problematic for ESL and developmental writing students, while the final chapter provides further practice. The first eleven chapters may be used in any order, and the final chapter may be drawn on as needed. It is possible to devote one week of class time to each chapter; however, depending on students' accuracy with each concept, there is enough material in the book when it is used as a supplemental text in a reading or writing class to fill a semester-long course.

Each of the first eleven chapters is composed of four sections. First, students develop an awareness of the grammar concept by reading a brief description, testing their prior knowledge with sentence-level items, and noticing how the grammar point is used in a brief piece of writing. The following section includes grammar explanations. When explanations are broken into subtopics, each subtopic ends with a short, sentence-level Self Check, which enables students to verify their understanding of the subtopic before moving to the next one. Charts and examples are used extensively to illustrate and visually reinforce the grammar points.

The exercises in the Editing Practice section focus on the task of editing discourse—a skill students need to apply in their own writing. The exercises move students from the sentence to the discourse level, and from more guided to less guided tasks. Exercise 1, like the Pretest, asks students to locate errors in sentence-level items. Exercises 2–4 provide paragraph-level editing practice based on adapted student writing. In Exercise 2, errors are pointed out for the student to correct; Exercise 3 generally requires students to supply the correct form of a given word; Exercise 4 asks students to locate and correct grammar errors in an unmarked piece of writing. Students are always told how many errors they must identify; however, just as in their own writing, they must scrutinize all sentences in order to edit the piece successfully. The exercises are appropriate for homework, in-class practice, or quizzes.

Each chapter ends with Writing Topics. Before students begin to write, they can read a sample paragraph based on one of the two guided writing tasks in the chapter. The sample paragraph not only models one of the writing topics, but also provides students with an example of a paragraph with a topic sentence, a body consisting of supporting sentences, and a concluding sentence. Once students have studied the expectations described in each writing topic, they can easily move to writing their own paragraph and editing for the grammatical structures presented in the chapter. The writing topics, designed for paragraph writing, are based on themes that are accessible to all students without instruction on the content.

Chapter 12 consists of paragraph-level editing exercises that are similar to Exercise 4 in the earlier chapters. However, these paragraphs require students to edit for more than one type of grammar error at a time, providing them with further realistic practice.

The first appendix, Practice with Authentic Language, contains excerpts from published writing. In this exercise, students practice their editing skills by selecting the correct form from alternatives. The next seven appendices offer students a reference guide to irregular verbs, subject-verb agreement, punctuation, preposition use, phrasal verbs, problem words and phrases, and commonly used correction symbols. The editing log found in Appendix 9 asks students to record and correct their grammar mistakes in an effort to help them become aware of the errors they make most frequently. Appendix 10 is a correlation between grammar topics presented in *Grammar for Writing 2: An Editing Guide to Writing* and *Fundamentals of English Grammar, Fourth Edition, Understanding and Using English Grammar, Fourth Edition,* and *Focus on Grammar 4, Fourth Edition*. The final appendix is a list of vocabulary used in each chapter that comes from the Academic Word List. An online answer key is also available.

Collaborative and Oral Activities

Grammar for Writing 2: An Editing Guide to Writing lends itself to individual work but is easily adapted to include more communicative activities. Suggestions for collaborative and oral activities include the following:

- After students take the Pretest, ask them to predict the grammar rules for the chapter.

- Have students work with a partner to read the paragraph following the Pretest. Together they can locate the target structures.

- Ask pairs of students to create editing exercises based on their own writing, focusing on the target structures.

- Ask students to submit samples of a target error from their own writing for the development of more exercises.

- Ask students to read their original paragraphs or exercises aloud to a partner to listen for grammatical correctness.

- Ask students to read their partner's writing aloud so that the writers can hear what they have written and check for errors.

- Ask a small group of students to develop a lesson about or an explanation of one grammar topic and present it to the class.

- Have partners, small groups, or the entire class discuss the sample paragraph in the Writing Topics section. Ask them to locate the topic sentence, major and minor supporting points, and concluding sentence.

- Have partners, small groups, or the entire class participate in a brainstorming session about the writing topics. This will help students develop ideas before they begin the writing assignment.

- Ask students to work collaboratively on the paragraph writing assignments and submit a collective group paragraph.

- Ask pairs or small groups to look at pieces of published writing and find examples of the target grammatical structures.

- Have a class discussion on the rhetorical features seen in the pieces of published writing in Appendix 1.

- Have students use the academic words found in Appendix 11 as they develop their collaborative work.

To the Student

Grammar for Writing 2: An Editing Guide to Writing presents the rules and practice you need to become a better writer and better editor of your writing. This book has a number of features that will help you accomplish these goals.

GRAMMAR TOPICS: The grammar topics in *Grammar for Writing 2: An Editing Guide to Writing* have been chosen based on an analysis of student writing. The errors you will focus on are ones that student writers make often and need to correct. Through practice, you will begin to find, correct, and eventually eliminate these common errors in your own writing.

BRIEF EXPLANATIONS: The brief, clear grammar explanations will help you focus on the key points that you need to edit your own work successfully. The charts and appendices provide handy tools for quick reference.

STUDENT WRITING: Most exercises are developed from student writing. Therefore, the exercises reflect topics and grammar points that are relevant to student writers.

SEQUENCE OF EXERCISES: The pretests help you assess your knowledge of each grammar topic and decide how much practice you need. The subsequent sample paragraphs and exercises in each chapter become progressively more difficult, allowing you to build skills and confidence as you work through the exercises. Finally, you are given the chance to produce and edit your own writing.

EXTRA EDITING: In general, when you edit your own writing, you will be looking for various types of errors, not just one type. Therefore, in Chapter 12, you will have additional practice editing for more than one error type in each exercise.

PUBLISHED WRITING: It is always helpful to notice how professional writers use the language. The Practice with Authentic Language exercises in Appendix 1 are drawn from published articles. They will allow you to become more aware of the structures used by professional writers in published material.

EDITING LOG: The editing log found in Appendix 9 will help you focus on the grammar errors that you make most frequently. By recording the grammar mistakes that your teacher finds in your paragraphs and essays, you will begin to see a pattern of certain errors. Once you know your grammar weaknesses, you can successfully edit for and eliminate them in future writing.

ACADEMIC WORD LIST: The list of academic words found in Appendix 11 is based on the words that are frequently used in college- and university-level writing. These are the words that you will need to know and be able to use to be a successful college student. As you work through the exercises in each chapter, locate the academic words and notice how they are used; then, practice using some of these words as you write on your own.

Acknowledgments

Many thanks to the students who have made *Grammar for Writing 2: An Editing Guide to Writing* possible, beginning with my former students at the University of California, Irvine and continuing with my current students at Fullerton College. It is their desire for accurate writing that has guided this book.

Many more thanks to the Pearson ELT editors and staff who have helped me navigate through the publishing process. I owe a great deal to Massimo Rubini, Paula Van Ells, Stacey Hunter, Kathy Furgang, and Marian Wassner, whose perceptive, accurate, and detailed suggestions have helped in the creation of this book. In addition, my colleagues at the University of California, Irvine and Fullerton College have been both helpful and supportive throughout this process. I thank them sincerely.

Finally, I want to thank my family, especially my husband, Paul, whose continued enthusiasm for this project has never waivered.

Tenses and Time Shifts

GRAMMAR FOCUS

Knowing how to form the twelve verb tenses and when to use each of them to express present, past, and future time will help you write more clearly. Once you understand each tense, you will be able to shift between these time frames appropriately. In the following sections, you will review the form and use of the verb tenses as well as guidelines for using time shifts in your writing.

Pretest

Check your understanding of verb tenses. Put a check (✓) next to the sentences that are correct.

____ **1.** Michael ran when he twisted his ankle.

____ **2.** The train running on time right now, but it hadn't been running on time before rush hour.

____ **3.** The university has been offering this course since 1997.

____ **4.** Because of all the phone calls I've made this month, my phone bill will be larger than usual.

____ **5.** We had seen all the DVDs at home, so now we have to rent some.

____ **6.** We will not be going to the lecture this evening.

____ **7.** The tour group will have travel the entire southern coast by the end of the trip.

____ **8.** Professor Milton is teaching at the college for many years.

____ **9.** Mr. Duong will has been working here for a year by the end of next month.

____ **10.** Lynda and Amy had been searching the library for an hour before they found the books they needed.

Notice how the following paragraph uses different verb tenses. Some of the verbs are underlined. Circle the time word that identifies the tense for each underlined verb.

Modern organic farming is the result of advances <u>made</u> during the twentieth century. Before World War II, advances in engineering and biochemistry <u>had changed</u> traditional farming methods. However, the heavy use of fertilizers and pesticides after World War II <u>brought about</u> an international interest in green or organic farming methods. While most research <u>was still focusing</u> on new chemicals to improve farming, Rachel Carson <u>published</u> *Silent Spring* in 1962. Some people believe this book started the environmental movement. Since that time, governments around the world <u>have been setting</u> standards for the use of chemicals in farming and certification of organic products. Because organics <u>have become</u> so popular over the past decades, large corporate farmers <u>are currently entering</u> this business. Now that organic agriculture is common in the marketplace, the future struggle <u>will become</u> how to save the small farmers who were the founders of the original organic industry.

FORMING PRESENT VERBS

Regular Verbs in the Present

The following chart shows the forms of regular verbs in the present.

	SUBJECT	VERB	
Simple Present	I/You/We/They	leave/do not leave	at 5:00 P.M.
	He/She/It	leaves/does not leave	
Present Progressive	I	am (not) taking	a long time.
	You/We/They	are (not) taking	
	He/She/It	is (not) taking	
Present Perfect	I/You/We/They	have (not) arrived	on time.
	He/She/It	has (not) arrived	
Present Perfect Progressive	I/You/We/They	have (not) been working	for three hours.
	He/She/It	has (not) been working	

Be, Have, and *Do* in the Present

Some common verbs are irregular in the simple present.

SUBJECT	BE	
I	**am (not)**	
He/She/It	**is (not)**	in the office.
You/We/They	**are (not)**	

SUBJECT	HAVE	
I/You/We/They	**have/do not have**	enough water.
He/She/It	**has/does not have**	

SUBJECT	DO	
I/You/We/They	**do/do not do**	good work.
He/She/It	**does/does not do**	

USING PRESENT VERBS

1. The simple present is used to describe or write about:

- general truths or facts

  It **takes** *five hours to fly from California to New York.*

- habits or routines

  Louise **takes** *the bus to school every day.*

- books or movies

  In the novel When I Was Puerto Rican, *Negi* **moves** *from Puerto Rico to New York and eventually* **enrolls** *at Harvard University.*

2. The present progressive is used to describe or write about:

- current actions or states

  Preston **is studying** *for his test.*

- current actions over an extended time period

  Darlene **is majoring** *in East Asian Studies.*

3. The present perfect is used to describe or write about:

- actions that began in the past and continue in the present

    Mrs. Alvarez **has lived** here since 1966.

- recently completed actions that affect the present

    I**'ve** just **finished** a very difficult exam, so I'm exhausted.

- actions or events that happened at an unspecified time in the past

    They **have seen** that show before.

4. The present perfect progressive is used to:

- describe or write about actions that began in the past and continue to the present

    We **have been waiting** for a long time.

- emphasize the duration of actions that began in the past and have continued to the present

    We **have been waiting** to board the plane for two hours.

NOTE: The present perfect and present perfect progressive have no difference in meaning with verbs of occupation and living.

The Alden family **has lived** in the United States for three generations.

The Alden family **has been living** in the United States for three generations.

Farah **has worked** for the State Department since 1998.

Farah **has been working** for the State Department since 1998.

Using Time Words in the Present

Use time words to indicate different forms of the present.

SIMPLE PRESENT	PRESENT PROGRESSIVE	PRESENT PERFECT	PRESENT PERFECT PROGRESSIVE
always, every day/week/month/year, never, often, rarely, seldom, usually	at present, at this moment, nowadays, right now, this week/month/year, today	already, always, for, just, recently, several/many times, since, so far, this week/month/year, until now, yet	all day/week/month/year, by now, for, since, so far, this week/month/year, up to now

Self Check 1

Circle the sentence that uses the correct present verb form.

1. (a) Most basketball players have been tall.

(b) Most basketball players are tall. ✓

2. (a) We haven't sent our tax payment yet this year. ✓

(b) We haven't send our tax payment yet this year.

3. (a) This semester I take four classes.

(b) This semester I am taking four classes. ✓

4. **(a)** We have been studying for the exam since last Friday.

   (b) We are studying for the exam <u>since</u> last Friday.

5. **(a)** Students register for classes for a week so far.

   (b) Students have been registering for classes for a week <u>so far</u>.

FORMING PAST VERBS

Regular Verbs in the Past

The following chart shows the forms of regular verbs in the past.

	SUBJECT	VERB	
Simple Past	I/You/He/She/It/We/They	**looked/did not look**	good yesterday.
Past Progressive	You/We/They	**were (not) driving**	to work at one o'clock.
	I/He/She/It	**was (not) driving**	
Past Perfect	I/You/He/She/It/We/They	**had (not) entered**	the train station before the rain storm.
Past Perfect Progressive	I/You/He/She/It/We/They	**had (not) been repeating**	the same formula for an hour before class.

for several hours
in progress.

Irregular Verbs in the Past

The verb *be* has two forms in the simple past.

SUBJECT	BE	
I/He/She/It	**was**	in London last month.
You/We/They	**were**	

Some other common verbs that are irregular in the simple past are:

break — **broke**	*grow* — **grew**
bring — **brought**	*have* — **had**
do — **did**	*let* — **let**
find — **found**	*put* — **put**
get — **got**	*see* — **saw**
go — **went**	

NOTE: All irregular verbs except *be* have the same simple past form for all subjects.

USING PAST VERBS

1. The simple past is used to describe or write about:

   - actions or situations that began and ended at a specific time in the past

     Alvin **graduated** *last June.*

     Bob **was** *sick two days ago.*

   - habitual past actions

     We **ate** *at this restaurant every Friday night for years.*

   NOTE: *Used to or would are also used to refer to habitual past actions. Used to emphasizes a contrast with the present and is more common than would.*

   We **used to ride** *our bikes to school when we were children.*

   I **would ride** *my bike to school every day before I got my driver's license.*

2. The past progressive is used to describe or write about:

   - actions in progress at a specific time in the past

     I **was studying** *in the library at nine o'clock last night.*

   - an action in progress that is interrupted by another action

     Lan **was talking** *on the phone when the pizza delivery arrived.*

   - two past actions in progress at the same time

     While Hala **was barbecuing** *the fish, her husband* **was making** *the salad.*

3. The past perfect is used to describe or write about a past action or event that happened or existed before another past action or time.

   In Rome, we saw the sites that we **had read** *about in our history books.*

   My sister **had done** *all the housework by noon.*

   NOTE: When only one past action or event is mentioned in a sentence, use the simple past, not the past perfect.

   We **drove** *home in the rain last night.*

                              not

   We had driven home in the rain last night.

4. The past perfect progressive is used to describe or write about an action or event that was in progress before or until another time or event. The past perfect progressive is often used to express the duration of the first event or action.

   Celeste **had been working** *on the project for two months when the company decided to cancel it.*

Using Time Words in the Past

Use time words to indicate different forms of the past.

SIMPLE PAST	PAST PROGRESSIVE	PAST PERFECT	PAST PERFECT PROGRESSIVE
a few minutes ago, in 1990, in the past, last week, the day before yesterday, yesterday	as, at that time/ moment, at the time, during, in the 1950s/1990s, when	after, before, by the time, by then, for, since, until, when	at that moment, at that time, by that time, by then, since

Self Check 2

Circle the sentence that uses the correct past verb form.

1. (a) James broke the mirror when he dropped it. ✓

   (b) James breaked the mirror when he dropped it.

2. (a) Connie was not very tired last night. ✓

   (b) Connie had not been very tired last night.

3. (a) I didn't recognize Neha at the party because I've not seen her for ten years.

   (b) I didn't recognize Neha at the party because I had not seen her for ten years. ✓

4. (a) Caleb studied when I called him.

   (b) Caleb was studying when I called him. ✓

5. (a) The sun had been shining for several hours before it started to rain. ✓

   (b) The sun had been shine for several hours before it started to rain.

FORMING FUTURE VERBS

	SUBJECT	VERB	
Simple Future	I/You/He/She/It/We/They	will (not) arrive	later today.
be going to	I	am (not) going to move	
	You/We/They	are (not) going to move	next summer.
	He/She/It	is (not) going to move	
Future Progressive	I/You/He/She/It/We/They	will (not) be working	tomorrow.
Future Perfect	I/You/He/She/It/We/They	will (not) have left	by five o'clock.
Future Perfect Progressive	I/You/He/She/It/We/They	will (not) have been working	for several hours by the time the sun rises.

USING FUTURE VERBS

1. The simple future is used to describe or write about actions, events, or states that will occur in the future, including:

   - scheduled events

     The movie **will begin** *at 8:30.*

   - predictions

     Will *it* **be** *sunny tomorrow? It probably* **will be.**

   - promises

     Maddie **will** *never* **tell** *your secret.*

   - offers

     We **will drive** *you to school tomorrow.*

   NOTE: In speech *will* is often contracted when used for offers.

   *We***'ll drive** *you to school tomorrow.*

   - decisions made at the moment of speaking

     *I think I***'ll take** *a walk.*

2. *Be going to* + verb is used to describe or write about:

   - planned events

     *We***'re going to work** *at the mall this summer.*

     I **am going to take** *five classes next semester.*

   - predictions

     I think this class **is going to be** *my favorite one.*

3. The future progressive is used to describe or write about an action that will be in progress at a time in the future.

   John and Kim **will be sailing** *on the lake all day Saturday.*

4. The future perfect is used to describe or write about a future action that will happen before another future action or time.

   You **will** *probably* **have left** *for the party by the time John arrives.*

   Laird and Paige **will have graduated** *by next June.*

5. The future perfect progressive is used to describe or write about future events or actions that continue up to another future event or time. The future perfect progressive is often used to express the duration of the first event or action.

   By the time you graduate, I **will have been working** *for several years.*

   We **will have been watching** *the tennis finals for an hour when you arrive at three o'clock.*

6. Like the simple future, the simple present can be used to describe or write about scheduled events.

   The bus **departs** *at six o'clock tomorrow morning.*

   The performance **begins** *at eight o'clock tonight.*

NOTE: Verbs commonly used in the simple present to refer to the future are: *arrive, begin, depart, finish, leave,* and *start.*

7. The present progressive can be used to describe or write about a previously arranged future action.

> We**'re leaving** *town tomorrow afternoon.*
>
> *Padma and Sabin* **are meeting** *for a golf game next Saturday.*

Using Time Words in the Future

Use time words to indicate different forms of the future.

SIMPLE FUTURE, *BE GOING TO* + VERB, FUTURE PROGRESSIVE	FUTURE PERFECT, FUTURE PERFECT PROGRESSIVE
the day after tomorrow, later, next week/month/year, tomorrow, tonight	by that time, by the time, by then, for

Self Check 3

Circle the sentence that uses the correct future verb form.

1. **(a)** Tomas and Ruben going to leave for Mexico tomorrow morning.

   (b) Tomas and Ruben are going to leave for Mexico tomorrow morning.

2. **(a)** Zach is a year old next summer.

   (b) Zach will be a year old next summer.

3. **(a)** Ria will wear her wedding gown for six hours by the end of the wedding celebration.

   (b) Ria will have been wearing her wedding gown for six hours by the end of the wedding celebration.

4. **(a)** The students think that the final exam next week is difficult.

   (b) The students think that the final exam next week is going to be difficult.

5. **(a)** We will be remodeling our house later this year.

   (b) We will remodeling our house later this year.

CHOOSING THE CORRECT TENSE

Good writers always choose the verb tense that most clearly conveys their meaning. Being aware of how different tenses can change your meaning will help you choose the most appropriate tense. The following section explains the differences between tenses that are often confused.

Present Time

The following three sentences refer to the present, but each one has a different meaning.

> *Joleen* **works** *at the bookstore.*

The simple present emphasizes the fact that the action is a habit or happens regularly, for example, *every Tuesday.*

*Joleen **is working** at the bookstore.*

The present progressive emphasizes the fact that the action is happening currently or for a temporary period of time, for example, *this week*.

*Joleen **has worked** at the bookstore since last summer.*

The present perfect emphasizes the period of time over which the event has occurred, for example, *from last summer to the present.*

Simple Past versus Present Perfect

The following two sentences refer to the past, but the exact time in the past is different.

*I **saw** the movie a few months ago.*

The simple past is used to describe an action that occurred at a specific time in the past.

*I'**ve seen** the movie before.*

The present perfect is used to describe an action that occurred at an unspecified time in the past.

Simple Past versus Past Progressive

The following two sentences refer to the past, but the exact time in the past is different.

*I **slept** well last night.*

The simple past is used to describe an action that occurred at a specific time in the past.

*I **was sleeping** when she **called**.*

The past progressive is used to describe an action that was happening in the past and was interrupted by a second action. The second action is in the simple past.

Simple Past versus Past Perfect

The following two sentences refer to the past, but the exact time in the past is different.

*He **cleaned** the apartment when his mother **arrived**.*

The simple past is used to describe two past actions that occurred at the same time.

*He **had cleaned** the apartment when his mother **arrived**.*

The past perfect is used to describe one past action that occurred before another past action. The second action that occurred is in the simple past.

Present Perfect versus Present Perfect Progressive

The following two sentences use perfect verb forms, but each one has a different meaning.

*Quincy **has read** the book.*

The present perfect shows that the action happened in the past one or more times.

*Quincy **has been reading** the book.*

The present perfect progressive emphasizes that the action is continuous and that it has not been completed.

Stative Verbs

- Some verbs have stative meanings. They describe states or situations that exist. These verbs are not usually used in the progressive tenses.

> Dov **knows** *most of the answers on the test.*

Other verbs with stative meanings include the following:

appreciate	exist	mind	prefer
believe	fear	need	realize
belong	hate	owe	recognize
care	like	own	understand
dislike	love	please	want

- Some verbs may have a stative meaning as well as a progressive meaning.

> Gerald **is weighing** *himself on the scale.*

The present progressive describes the action of standing on the scale and reading it.

> Gerald **weighs** *100 pounds.*

The simple present describes Gerald's state. There is no action.

> not
>
> *Gerald is weighing 100 pounds.*

Other verbs that can have both stative and progressive meanings include the following:

appear	imagine	smell
be	include	taste
feel	look	think
forget	remember	
have	see	

Self Check 4

Circle the sentence that uses the correct verb tense.

1. (a) George has been performing in the choir once last year.

   (b) George performed in the choir once last year.

2. (a) They are belonging to the Latin Club.

   (b) They belong to the Latin Club.

3. (a) The classroom felt very hot during the exam.

   (b) The classroom was feeling very hot during the exam.

4. (a) She has finished the project yesterday.

(b) She finished the project yesterday.

5. (a) I feel sick and have had a stomachache for an hour. I think I'll leave work early today.

(b) I feel sick and had a stomachache for an hour. I think I'll leave work early today.

USING TIME SHIFTS

Writers often shift between present, past, and future time within a piece of writing. Using the correct verb tenses lets readers easily understand when actions and events take place.

1. Remember that when you use a time word or phrase (*tomorrow, yesterday,* or *next month*), the verb tense must agree with it. When time is not directly mentioned, think carefully about the time you want to express and choose the correct tense.

2. Avoid unnecessary shifts in tense, but be aware that you will often need to use several different tenses in a piece of writing. The following example paragraph shows time shifts that are necessary in order for the writer to discuss the current situation and how it relates to past and future events. Notice how the verb tenses correspond to the related time words or phrases.

> *(1)* **This year** *the history department* **is requiring** *students with a history major to take a new four-unit course in their junior year. (2) This* **means** *that students* **now** **have to take** *forty units in history to graduate. (3)* **In previous years**, *the minimum* **was** *thirty-six units. (4) The department* **will review** *the program* **after one year.** **Then** *the department* **will decide** *whether or not it* **is going to keep** *this new requirement.*

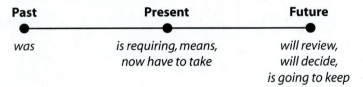

Past	Present	Future
was	is requiring, means, now have to take	will review, will decide, is going to keep

In this paragraph, the boldfaced verbs show a shift from the present to the past to the future. The writer shifts from a discussion of what is true in the present (*this year* and *now*) to what was true in the past (*previous years*) and finally to what will happen in the future (*after one year* and *then*). Shifting tenses is necessary to compare the situation now and in the past and to explain how it may change in the future.

WRITING TIP

Pay close attention to time shifts when you read for school or for pleasure. Notice how time words or phrases signal shifts in time.

In the following paragraph, the underlined verbs are not correct. Write the correct verb form above each underlined verb.

Last year we <u>spend</u> our vacation in the Caribbean. We relaxed in the sun

1

and read books while our children were playing in the warm ocean water.

Next summer we <u>drive</u> to the mountains to spend our vacation in a house

2

on a lake. We <u>planned</u> to stay there for one week. The following year, we will

3

have more time for our vacation, so we <u>consider</u> going somewhere farther   *have considered.*

4

away. Perhaps we <u>are going</u> to Europe.

5

will go

EDITING PRACTICE

1. *Put a check (✓) next to the sentences that use verb tenses and time shifts correctly. Correct the sentences that have errors. There may be more than one way to correct some errors.*

_____ **1.** Many people <u>are believing</u> that increased security has led to a loss of   *believe*

freedom in our country.

__✓__ **2.** We hope that the college will offer more music classes next semester.

_____ **3.** My seven-year-old son <u>has read</u> the first Harry Potter book last week.

_____ **4.** The audience will have been <u>waiting</u> in line for two hours by the time   *waited*

the movie begins.

_____ **5.** I think it <u>is raining</u> tomorrow.   *will be*

_____ **6.** When my parents and I got to the reunion, our extended family <u>has</u>

arrived.   *had*

_____ **7.** Professor Xu <u>was finishing</u> his final lecture when the students began to   *finished*

applaud.

_____ **8.** According to the schedule, we <u>will have been writing</u> an essay every   *write*

week of the upcoming term.

_____ **9.** By the time the semester ends, the class <u>will have learned</u> to write strong

thesis statements and good topic sentences.

_____ **10.** Last week the Whaling Museum was showing *~~showed~~* a film on the whale ship

The Essex, and the week before, it had showing the children's movie *Free*

Willy.

✓ **11.** Virginia and Louis have been dating for two years.

_____ **12.** She reads *has read* that book four times so far.

2. *Read the following paragraph. Complete the paragraph with the correct forms of the verbs.*

Exercises that focus on reducing stress such as yoga, tai chi,

and meditation ___*have become*___ popular recently.
       1. become / have become

Another way to reduce stress that isn't discussed a lot, but one that I

find especially helpful, is fishing. Like yoga, tai chi, and meditation,

fishing is relaxing, but it also has many other benefits that most people

___*are*___ not aware of. Throughout time, many
      2. were / are

fisherman ___*see*___ fishing as a form of fun and
      3. see / have seen

leisure. While they ___*are waiting*___ for the "big one,"
      4. waited / are waiting

they have time to think about life and to forget their problems. This is also

true for me, but the time that I ___*have spent*___ with
      5. had spent / have spent

my dad, family, and friends while fishing over the past twenty years is also

very important. I started fishing with my dad when I was a child, and I

___*have been fishing*___ ever since. Before I held a fishing pole,
      6. have been fishing / fished

I ___*had spent*___ hours watching my dad while he was
      7. had spent / have spent

fishing. When I was old enough to fish, I ___*used to come*___
      8. used to come / would to come

home with the biggest and the most fish. However, now I

___*prefer*___ the relaxation of fishing more than the
      9. prefer / am preferring

result. Another benefit of this sport is that a person can do it for his or her

entire life. Because of this, I have begun looking forward to the time that I

will have gone fishing with my children and grandchildren. With
10. **will go fishing / will have gone fishing**
all of these benefits associated with fishing, it's surprising that more people

are not taking up the sport.

3. *In the following paragraph, the underlined verbs are not correct. Write the correct form above each underlined verb. There may be more than one way to correct some errors.*

Rage is an emotion that people of all ages and all nationalities feel. It is

an emotion that <u>was</u> very hard to ignore. Even if someone tries to control his
₁

or her rage, many times it <u>has still surfaced</u>. Violent actions or insulting
₂

words are both results of rage. Another type of rage that we <u>hear</u> about over
₃

the past years is road rage. Sometimes people <u>entered</u> a roadway and see
₄

drivers who are yelling at each other over small accidents or during traffic

jams. People <u>are seeming</u> to have quick tempers as a result of small
₅

frustrations. Themes of rage have also appeared in modern literature. In the

short story "Like a Winding Sheet" by Ann Petry, Mr. Johnson controls the

anger he feels at work. However, his anger eventually <u>turned</u> to rage inside of
₆

him. He <u>is arriving</u> at home and immediately releases his rage on his wife.
₇

This story <u>has ended</u> tragically; sadly, similar consequences of rage <u>became</u>
₈ ₉

more frequent in real life. People need to control this emotion; otherwise,

we, our children, and our children's children <u>will have experienced</u> many
₁₀

frightening and unnecessary consequences of rage in the future.

4. *The following paragraph has ten errors in the use of verb tenses. Find and correct the errors. There may be more than one way to correct some errors.*

It seems that many teenagers looked at driving as a right rather than as

a privilege that they are having to earn. In order for young adults to take this

privilege more seriously, many states recently change their laws so that it is

harder for teens to get a driver's license. I believe this is a good change because

I have saw many dangerous incidents with teenage

drivers since I had gotten my license five years ago.

I know that I was part of the problem when I was

a new driver, and I am in many near accidents.

However, I was lucky. In order to keep everyone

safe, I think that parents and lawmakers should

prohibit teenagers below the age of eighteen

from driving at night, with friends, and on freeways. Most unsafe driving

seemed to occur when one of these factors is present. To make the restrictions

easier on teens, some cities have been improve their public transportation

systems. Though it will have been difficult for rural areas to expand public

transportation, these improvements and the changes in laws will keep drivers

safer than they are now. Teenage drivers may be upset at first, but if the

changes are made, everyone is safer in the future.

WRITING TOPICS

Study this student paragraph that uses different tenses and time words. Underline the verbs and circle the time words that indicate a change in time frame.

Most academic paragraphs, whether they are part of an essay or stand alone, include a clear topic sentence, a body, and a concluding sentence. Notice that this paragraph has these three important parts of an academic paragraph. Use this paragraph as a model when you write about one of the topics on page 18.

Because earthquakes are a common occurrence in Japan, the Japanese people have learned to prepare for them. In the past, many areas of the country experienced a large number of deaths and extensive destruction from earthquakes. For example, in 1923 an earthquake near Tokyo killed 100,000 people, and in 1995 an earthquake near Kobe killed 6,000 people and destroyed 100,000 homes. Recently, three important factors have lessened some of the problems associated with earthquakes in Japan. First of all, the government plays a very important role in the country's earthquake preparation. Since the late 1960s, the government has required modern building standards that stop buildings from collapsing during earthquakes. The government has also demanded that old buildings be retrofitted, which makes them stronger during earthquakes. Besides the government, the Japanese people have prepared for earthquakes over the past few decades. Most people

have earthquake survival kits that contain emergency supplies. They have also learned the importance of making plans with family members in case of an earthquake. Finally, scientists have been trying to develop an accurate way to detect future earthquakes. The methods that they use have been helpful, but they are not perfect yet. Most scientists believe that they will have an accurate earthquake predictor within the next decade. Although the Japanese government, people, and scientists have made many advances in the last forty years, devastating earthquakes such as the one on March 11, 2011 still cause widespread death and destruction. Therefore, being prepared for the future is going to remain a top priority for the country of Japan.

Choose one of the topics below and write at least one paragraph. Think carefully about the verb tenses you choose and the time shifts you make. After you complete your first draft, concentrate on editing your work. Keep in mind the editing practice from this chapter.

1. Throughout life, people set goals for themselves. Describe the goals you have had in the past and the goals you currently have. Think about these questions as you write. Which goals have you achieved? How did you achieve these goals? Why did you achieve some goals and not others? What could someone learn about you by knowing the goals you have set for yourself?

2. As technology has become more advanced, people are able to prepare for some natural disasters such as hurricanes, blizzards, and tornados. Describe what people do in an area of the world that you are familiar with when bad weather is approaching or a natural disaster occurs. What did they do in the past that was helpful or not helpful, and what can they do now to avoid problems associated with natural disasters?

Go to page 140 for more practice with verb tenses and time shifts.

Modals

GRAMMAR FOCUS

Modals such as *should, would,* and *must* and phrasal modals such as *be able to, be supposed to,* and *have to* are used in both the present/future and the past to express ideas such as ability, necessity, or possibility. In this chapter, you will learn both the meaning and the grammar of modals to make your writing as accurate as possible.

Pretest

Check your understanding of modals. Put a check (✓) next to the sentences that are correct.

_____ **1.** Julie must have fixed her computer because it is working now.

_____ **2.** Christopher could of gotten a better time in the triathlon, but he isn't a very strong swimmer.

_____ **3.** Rashid is such a good pianist today because he could have practiced for hours as a child.

_____ **4.** Criminology majors usually find jobs within the justice system, but they might have found jobs in education, too.

_____ **5.** They had better meet the next deadline on their project.

_____ **6.** Justine should study last night, but she went to the movies instead.

_____ **7.** Family possessions may have special significance to some and have no significance to others.

_____ **8.** May you tell me the time?

_____ **9.** We were supposed to study before we went out for the evening.

_____ **10.** It will be expensive, but we would go to Tahiti next summer.

Notice how the following paragraph uses present and past forms of modals.
Underline the modals in the present and circle the modals in the past.

In the United States, the disability rights movement began in the 1970s after the civil rights and women's rights movements. The goal of this movement was to improve the quality of life for people with disabilities. Before this time, many Americans would discriminate against the disabled. They believed that people with disabilities were not able to contribute to society. The disabled had to change the belief that their lives were worth less than others' lives. One of the first changes they fought for was easy access to buildings, public streets, and public transportation. The physically disabled could not use many public spaces until wheelchair ramps and elevators were added. In addition to the physical environment, equal opportunities in employment, education, and housing were necessary. Because of the success of the disability rights movement, disabled people are supposed to have the same opportunities as all others in society today. Although much progress has been made since the 1970s, more work must still be done so that people with disabilities will be able to lead completely equal lives.

FORMING MODALS

Present / Future

1. Use modal + base form of the verb to form the present or future of modals.

    Mark **can read** *Russian.*

    Drivers **must wear** *seatbelts at all times.*

2. For negatives, use modal + *not* + base form of the verb.

    Mark **cannot read** *Spanish.*

    Students **should not walk** *into class late.*

3. Modals do not have different forms for different subjects and are never followed by *to*.

    Jill **could drive** *him to school.*

    not

    Jill could drives him to school.

    Brandon **should arrive** *after everyone else.*

    not

    Brandon should to arrive after everyone else.

Past

1. Use modal + *have* + past participle to form the past of most modals.

    It **may have rained** *last night.*

    We **should have drunk** *more water before yesterday's hike.*

2. Use modal + *not* + *have* + past participle to form the negative past of modals.

> Marty **might not have gotten** *an A on the last exam.*
>
> *I* **should not have skipped** *class yesterday.*

WRITING TIP

In spoken English, the contraction for *have* sounds like the preposition *of*. Don't confuse the two in your writing.

*He could***'ve been** *a doctor.*

NOT

He could of been a doctor.

---

3. The past of *can* is *could* when showing ability.

> *Dr. McManus* **can speak** *two languages fluently now.*
>
> *As a child, Dr. McManus* **could speak** *three languages fluently.*

4. To form the past of phrasal modals (e.g., *be able to, be supposed to, have to*), use the simple past of the verb *be* or *have*. These verbs must agree with their subjects.

> *We* **were able to see / were not able to see** *the city lights as the plane flew over San Francisco.*
>
> *The doctor said Esther* **was supposed to exercise / was not supposed to exercise** *in gym class today.*
>
> *Donald and Di* **had to leave / didn't have to leave** *this morning.*

WRITING TIP

Maybe is an adverb that means *perhaps* or *possibly*. Be careful not to confuse it with the modal *may* + *be*.

Maybe *we will go out tonight.* (adverb)

We **may be** *at the restaurant before you arrive.* (may + be)

Self Check 1

Circle the sentence that uses the correct modal form.

1. **(a)** William and his brother should of traveled with us last summer.

   (b) William and his brother should have traveled with us last summer.

2. **(a)** Andrea may travels to Italy for spring break.

   (b) Andrea may travel to Italy for spring break.

3. **(a)** Josh should have not written that letter to his girlfriend.

   (b) Josh should not have written that letter to his girlfriend.

4. **(a)** Robin and Megan could play the piano when they were young.

   (b) Robin and Megan could played the piano when they were young.

5. **(a)** Norman didn't have to work yesterday because it was a holiday.

   (b) Norman had not to work yesterday because it was a holiday.

USING MODALS

MEANING	PRESENT	FUTURE	PAST
Showing Ability	can		could
	be able to	will be able to	was/were able to
	I **can lift** fifty pounds.		Last year I **could lift** 100 pounds.
	She **is able to run** a marathon.	She **will be able to come** tomorrow.	She **wasn't able to come** yesterday.
Making Requests	can	can	
	could	could	
	would	would	
	Can you **help** me now?	**Could** you **cook** dinner next week?	
Showing Possibility	can	can	
	may	may	may have
	might	might	might have
	could	could	could have
	He **might change** his major.	We **may leave** tomorrow.	I **could have left** earlier yesterday, but I didn't.
Showing Near Certainty *(deduction)*	must		must have
	He looks awful today; he **must be** sick.		It **must have rained** last night. The ground is wet.
Asking for and Giving Permission	can	can	
	could	could	
	may	may	
	May I **ask** you a question?	You **can use** my car on Saturday.	
Showing Necessity	must	must	
	have to	have to	had to
	We **must invite** the new neighbors to our party.	Do you **have to work** tomorrow?	She **had to take** the medicine last month.

MEANING	PRESENT	FUTURE	PAST
Showing Prohibition	**must not**	**must not**	
	cannot	**cannot**	
	Drivers **cannot turn** right at this intersection.	They **must not get** help on the next take-home exam.	
Showing Lack of Necessity	**do not + have to**	**do not + have to/will not + have to**	**did not + have to**
	You **do not have to take** the exam.	We **will not have to go** next time.	They **did not have to answer** the question.
Giving Advice / Making Suggestions	**had better (not)**	**had better (not)**	**had better (not) have**
	should	**should**	**should have**
	ought to	**ought to**	**ought to have**
	could	**could**	**could have**
	can	**can**	
	We **had better not be** late for the meeting!	You **had better leave** early tomorrow.	She **ought to have** taken Spanish 1 before Spanish 2.
	You **can borrow** that book from the library.		
Showing Expectation	**be supposed to**	**be supposed to**	**was/were supposed to**
	We **are supposed to be** in class right now.	They **are supposed to study** tonight.	You **were supposed to have left** yesterday.
Showing Preference	**would rather**	**would rather**	**would rather have**
	He **would rather write** an essay than take a test.	She **would rather start** school next fall than next spring.	He **would rather have eaten** dessert first.
Repeated Past Action			**would**
			When he was younger, he **would read** the same book over and over again.

(handwritten note next to Future column of "Showing Lack of Necessity": ← need to)

In spoken English, the modal *had better* is often shortened to *better*. This is acceptable in speaking but not in writing.

Spoken English:

The class **better** prepare for the upcoming exam.

Written English:

The class **had better** prepare for the upcoming exam.

Self Check 2

Circle the sentence that uses the correct modal.

1. (a) Because of the surgery, he is not supposed to eat fatty foods like French fries.

   (b) Because of the surgery, he doesn't have to eat fatty foods like French fries.

2. (a) Kelcie wasn't at the party last night, but she may have been because we had a good time.

   (b) Kelcie wasn't at the party last night, but she should have been because we had a good time.

3. (a) May you call me at home tonight?

   (b) Would you call me at home tonight?

4. (a) We're not sure where they went last night, but they could have been at the movies.

   (b) We're not sure where they went last night, but they would have been at the movies.

5. (a) The final project was due at eight o'clock yesterday morning. I must have completed it to pass the class.

   (b) The final project was due at eight o'clock yesterday morning. I had to complete it to pass the class.

EDITING PRACTICE

1. *Put a check (✓) next to the sentences that form and use modals correctly. Correct the sentences that have errors.*

   _____ 1. People must have calcium in their diets to have strong bones.

   _____ 2. Coach Arnold should have been a fast swimmer since she was in the Olympics.

   _____ 3. They closed all the shutters so that they could have seen the movie better.

____ 4. Elbert got an A on the exam. He must have studied a lot.

____ 5. Paul can fixes anything in the house.

____ 6. The flight should have took three hours, but there were delays at the

airport.

____ 7. You would receive a B on the exam in order to pass the course.

should

____ 8. Jenna had to buy a new car because her old one broke down so often.

____ 9. Shinna was suppose to teach in Japan last summer, but he didn't.

____ 10. We ought to have listened to our parents more often.

____ 11. Medical interns can practice not until they get their licenses.

____ 12. Zeke can be able to play on the varsity tennis team.

2. *Read the following paragraph. Choose the modal that best completes each sentence and write it on the line.*

Team sports _____ one of the best ways

1. **may be / may have been**

for children to learn teamwork and the importance of following directions.

Very few childhood activities require as much

cooperation as team sports. When children are on a

team, they _____

2. **must / have**

to listen to directions, work with their teammates,

and try not to blame others when things don't work

according to plan. Before children begin playing

sports, they _____

3. **may not work / may not have worked**

with others and _____ the skill of working

4. **may not learn / may not have learned**

as part of a group. Children _____

5. **have to follow / must have followed**

directions at school, but at school they are working for themselves, not

the group. Parents _____ these skills at

6. **may teach / would teach**

home, but children _____ carefully until

7. **might not listen / should not listen**

their peers and coaches are involved. The only drawback to team sports

_____ the parents. Some parents become
        8. should be / can be /

overly emotional at their children's sporting events. Perhaps these parents

_____ / playing group sports so that they
        9. should begin / are supposed to begin /

_____ the same lessons of teamwork and
        10. ought to learn / can learn /

cooperation that their children are learning.

3. *In the following paragraphs, the underlined modal and verb combinations
   are not correct. Write the correct modal above each underlined modal-verb
   combination. There may be more than one way to correct the errors.*

There is an old Chinese fable about good luck and bad luck. In the fable,

an old farmer lost his only horse. The other farmers in his village <u>must feel</u> *may*
                                                                        1

would take
horrible for him because all that they <u>would have talked</u> about was his bad
                                            2

luck. However, all that the old farmer could say was, "Good luck, bad luck,

who knows?" A few days later, the runaway horse returned with two wild

                                            would rather ?
horses following it. The farmers in the village <u>had better be</u> happy for the
                                                    3

old farmer because they spoke only of his good luck. The old farmer simply

responded, "Good luck, bad luck, who knows?" While the old farmer's son

was training the two new horses, he broke his leg, and the other farmers

were again saddened by the old farmer's bad luck. All that the old farmer
would say?
<u>might say</u> was, "Good luck, bad luck, who knows?" Several days later, the
   4

emperor's soldiers marched through the village and took all the men and

boys to fight in the emperor's war. The old farmer's son was left behind

because of his broken leg. Once again the old farmer had good luck, but all he
                    v
<u>would have said</u> was, "Good luck, bad luck, who knows?"
   5

The old farmer in this Chinese fable has a good attitude about good
                    might have
and bad luck. We <u>must have</u> good luck one day, but the next day that
            might (may⁶ turn
good luck <u>would turn</u> to bad luck. The fable is probably telling us that we
            7

~~should not have taken~~ *do not have to* luck too seriously and that we ought to make the best
[8]

of our situation without relying on luck.

4. *The following paragraphs have ten errors in the use of modals. Find and correct the errors. There may be more than one way to correct the errors.*

It is possible that a single event can change a person's life. The event ~~should~~ *might* be small, but it can make such an impact that life is never the same again. This happened to Daniel "Rudy" Rutteiger, whose life story is told in the film *Rudy.* In the film, Rudy dreams of going to the University of Notre Dame and playing football, but he is small and isn't very smart. Therefore, Rudy's friends and family think that he should ~~to~~ be satisfied as a steel worker like his father and his brothers. For years, Rudy does not pursue his dream and works in the steel plant, until his best friend is killed in an accident there. After this, Rudy feels he better *to* do everything possible to attend Notre Dame and play football. Because of one event and a lot of hard work, Rudy is able get a college degree, become the subject of a major motion picture, and start a career as a popular motivational speaker. Other people's lives *may not* ~~must not~~ change as dramatically as Rudy's, but events such as learning to swim, learning a foreign language, or even learning to ride a motorcycle could have impacted *might impact* life in unexpected ways.

Like Rudy, I am *was* able to begin college last fall due to one event—my parents' decision to move to the United States. Because of this single event, I have to speak two languages, vote for whomever I choose, and work in any field I want. I don't think most of us realize the importance that one choice must make in life, but like Rudy's and my experiences show, one event is *is able to* supposed to make all the difference in the world.

WRITING TOPICS

Study this student paragraph that uses modals in the present and past. Underline the present modal forms and circle the past modal forms. Most academic paragraphs, whether they are part of an essay or stand alone, include a clear topic sentence, a body, and a concluding sentence. Notice that this paragraph has these three important parts of an academic paragraph. Use this paragraph as a model when you write about one of the topics below.

Peer pressure is a fact of life for every teenager. This was also true for me when I was in high school, but I eventually learned how to handle this problem. There were many times when my friends would pressure me to smoke cigarettes, ditch school, or drink alcohol. At first I was not able to say no because I did not want to lose my friends, and I was curious about these forbidden activities. I must have known at the time that it was wrong to do these things, but I lacked the confidence to say no. After a few times, I felt I could not act this way anymore. Therefore, I began to lie to my friends about being busy so that I didn't have to join them anymore. Finally, I learned that I could tell them the truth about how I felt. Now I know that I should not have lied about my feelings. This experience of handling peer pressure taught me a good lesson for the future. I must always be honest with others even if it is not easy to do. I learned that I would rather tell the truth than have to live with a lie.

Choose one of the topics below and write at least one paragraph. Use a variety of modals. After you complete your first draft, concentrate on editing your work. Keep in mind the editing practice from this chapter.

1. Everyone makes mistakes in life. Describe a time when you made a mistake and explain how you could have handled the situation differently. What should you have done to avoid the mistake? How are you a better person today because of this experience?

2. What do you do when a person asks you to do something you don't want to do? How can you be honest without hurting the other person's feelings? How have you handled this type of situation in the past? Should you have done something differently? If so, how will you deal with this kind of situation in the future?

Go to page 142 for more practice with modals.

Nouns and Determiners

GRAMMAR FOCUS

The four types of determiners that are used before nouns are articles (*a, an, the*), quantifiers (*many, a little*, etc.), demonstrative adjectives (*this, that, these, those*), and possessive adjectives (*my, your, his*, etc.). Although using determiners can be complicated, the following guidelines will help you use them correctly. Before applying these guidelines for determiners, you will need to know whether a noun is countable or uncountable. Therefore, the following sections provide instruction and practice with nouns as well as with determiners.

Pretest

Check your understanding of nouns and determiners. Put a check (✓) next to the sentences that are correct.

_____ **1.** Omar has a lot of confidences in himself.

_____ **2.** Please look at my homework. Did you get this answers for questions 10 through 15?

_____ **3.** He tested the three hypotheses and found that they were all correct.

_____ **4.** The news on television are always bad.

_____ **5.** I just finished a good book that I think you might like.

_____ **6.** Orange has a lot of vitamin C.

_____ **7.** Jake has to take a trash out tonight.

_____ **8.** Mr. and Mrs. Adams loved the foreign film that you recommended.

_____ **9.** This book doesn't have picture to help children understand the story.

_____ **10.** Each of the assignments is worth 10 percent of the total grade.

Notice how the following paragraph uses countable and uncountable nouns and determiners. Ten nouns are underlined. Discuss with a partner why some of the underlined nouns have determiners and others do not. Also, discuss why different determiners are used with each noun.

<u>Humans</u> have always had the ability to multitask or do several things at one time, but with the <u>amount</u> of electronic technology that is available nowadays, <u>multitasking</u> has become the subject of debate. Electronic gadgets have enabled people in the twenty-first century to do homework, talk on the phone, watch television, and work on the <u>computer</u> all at the same time. The <u>problem</u> with this kind of multitasking is that the possibility of errors increases and the time it takes to complete a <u>project</u> goes up. In addition, the brain normally needs time to rest between each <u>action</u>. To solve these <u>problems</u>, many researchers are now saying that people, especially <u>teenagers</u>, need time away from electronic media and the temptation to do several things at once. They can then focus on one <u>task</u>, including face-to-face communication with family and friends.

NOUNS

Count Nouns

1. Countable or count nouns are nouns that that can be counted. They have singular and plural forms. The plural is generally formed by adding *–s* or *–es*. Spelling changes are required in some cases.

    *ba**b**y — bab**ies***

    *computer — computer**s***

    *lea**f** — leav**es***

    *tomat**o** — tomato**es***

2. Some count nouns have irregular plural forms.

    *child — child**ren***

    *hypothes**is** — hypothes**es***

    *man — **men***

    *person — **people***

    *phenomen**on** — phenomen**a***

    *syllab**us** — syllab**i***

WRITING TIP
Refer to a dictionary if you are not certain of a plural form or you are using a noun for the first time.

3. Singular count nouns must always be preceded by a determiner.

> *Did you finish* **the** *project for* **your** *history teacher?*

the (a)   not

> *Did you finish project for history teacher?*

the

> *There hasn't been* **a** *person in* **the** *store all day.*

not

> *There hasn't been person in store all day.*

a   the

Uncountable Nouns

1. Uncountable or noncount nouns cannot generally be counted. They do not have plural forms. Some examples of uncountable nouns are:

information	love	news
intelligence	milk	

2. The indefinite articles *a* and *an* cannot be used with uncountable nouns.

> *There is* **pollution** *in all parts of the world.*

pollution.

or

> *There is* **some pollution** *in all parts of the world.*

a/an can't + [uc]

not

> *There is* **a** *pollution in all parts of the world.*

3. Many uncountable nouns can be placed into categories.

Abstract nouns or concepts: *adolescence, adulthood, advice, anger, behavior, confidence, courage, discrimination, diversity, education, evidence, fun, happiness, health, honesty, importance, information, knowledge, laughter, luck, news, patience, progress, proof, research, significance, time, transportation, violence, wealth*

Natural materials: *blood, dirt, dust, gold, ice, iron, paper, sand, silver, water*

Gases: *air, oxygen, pollution, smog, smoke, steam*

Natural occurrences: *electricity, fire, fog, light, rain, snow, sunshine, wind*

Foods: *bread, butter, cereal, cheese, fruit, lettuce, meat, pork, poultry, soup*

Liquids: *coffee, juice, milk, oil, tea, water, wine*

Fields of study: *biology, chemistry, economics, history, literature, mathematics, medicine, physics, politics*

Groups of similar items: *equipment, furniture, garbage, homework, jewelry, luggage, machinery, money, scenery, traffic, vocabulary, work*

NOTE: Uncountable nouns use singular verbs.

Anger is *a destructive emotion.*

Research has *uncovered many causes of cancer.*

4. Some nouns can be both countable and uncountable. Note how the meaning changes from general to specific when the uncountable noun becomes a count noun.

General liquid: *Many people drink* **coffee** *with breakfast.*

Specific serving: *I'd like two small* **coffees** *to go, please.*

General substance: *The building has large windows made of* **glass.**

Specific object: *I dropped the* **glasses** *and they broke.*

General food: *I'll go to the store and get some* **cheese.**

Specific type: *The shop sells forty different* **cheeses.**

WRITING TIP

If you are using a noun for the first time, always look in an ESL or learner's dictionary to find out if the noun is countable (C for countable) or uncountable (U for uncountable).

Self Check 1

Circle the sentence that uses count and uncountable nouns correctly.

1. **(a)** Brian got a new computer equipment last night.

   (b) Brian got new computer equipment last night.

2. **(a)** The violence in our city is getting worse every year.

   (b) The violences in our city are getting worse every year.

3. **(a)** We ordered three large tea.

   (b) We ordered three large cups of tea.

4. **(a)** Pam wrote an essay for her English class last night.

   (b) Pam wrote essay for her English class last night.

5. **(a)** Physics are my favorite subject.

   (b) Physics is my favorite subject.

ARTICLES

The Indefinite Articles *A* and *An*

1. Use *a* or *an* with singular count nouns that are not specifically identified or that express a general meaning.

> *Kiren and Ivar went to* **a concert** *last night.*

(We don't know which concert. It was one of any number of concerts.)

> *I had* **a bagel** *for breakfast.*

(We don't know which bagel, and it is not important to know which bagel.)

2. Use *a* or *an* with singular count nouns to make generalizations about people, objects, or concepts. A plural noun with no article conveys the same general meaning.

> **A new car** *must have* **an airbag.**

> or

> *New* **cars** *must have* **airbags.**

(All cars now have this requirement.)

3. Do not use *a* or *an* with uncountable nouns.

> *Amilia always has* **bad luck** *in Las Vegas.*

> not

> *Amilia always has a bad luck in Las Vegas.*

NOTE: *A* is used with nouns that begin with consonant sounds, while *an* is used with nouns that begin with vowel sounds.

> *The textbook has* **a** *discussion section at the end of each chapter.*

> *There is* **an** *Appalachian folk song on the radio.*

> **A** *university student must give up some of his or her leisure time to study.*

> (*University* begins with a consonant sound—"yuniversity.")

> *It is* **an** *honor to graduate with academic recognition.*

> (*Honor* begins with a vowel sound—"ahnor.")

The Definite Article *The*

1. Use *the* when a noun is mentioned for the second time and your reader is familiar with it. The first time a noun is mentioned, the indefinite article *a* or *an* is generally used.

> *Yesterday Kazuo got* **a speeding ticket** *when he was driving to school. He says that* **the ticket** *is going to cost over $200.*

2. Use *the* with count nouns and uncountable nouns to express specific meaning. The reader knows which person, object, or concept is being referred to. *The* is generally used when the noun is followed by an adjective clause or prepositional phrase, since the noun becomes specific with the description following it.

> **The concert** *was excellent.*

(Both the writer and reader know which concert is being referred to.)

> **The cars in our garage** *don't have air bags.*

(These are specific cars; they are the ones in our garage.)

> **The evidence that the police found** *is strong.*

(This is specific evidence—the evidence the police found.)

> *Do you have* **the instructions for our printer***?*

(Both the writer and the reader know which instructions are being referred to.)

3. Use *the* with singular count nouns to refer to a type of animal, invention, or currency but not a specific one.

> **The hawk** *is a bird of prey.*

> **The telephone** *was invented in the nineteenth century.*

> **The yen** *is the currency of Japan.*

4. Use *the* after an *of* phrase that shows quantity, for example:

> *all of the*

> *half of the*

> *more of the*

> *most of the*

> *one of the*

> *some of the*

> *I answered* **most of the** *questions on the exam.*

5. Use *the* + adjective (without a noun) to refer to a group of people, for example:

the Chinese	*the injured*
the dead	*the old*
the disabled	*the poor*
the elderly	*the rich*
the English	*the sick*
the French	*the unemployed*
the homeless	*the young*

> **The elderly** *should be treated with respect.*

> **The homeless** *need more understanding from society.*

6. Use *the* with superlatives, ordinal numbers, and the adjective *same.*

> *Jonah is* **the best** *student in our class.*

> *I liked the movie better* **the second** *time I saw it.*

> *Are you taking* **the same** *class as Karen?*

7. Some idiomatic expressions always use the article *the*.

> *Every day Ulla eats breakfast* **in the morning** *at seven o'clock and lunch* **in the afternoon** *at one o'clock, but she never eats dinner at night.*

> *We love to go* **to the movies/the beach/the park**.

> *They have to go* **to the bank/the store/the library**.

No Article or Zero Article (ø)

1. Use no article (ø) with plural count nouns and uncountable nouns to express a general meaning, an entire class of people or objects, and concepts.

> *Her father collects* **stamps**.

(He collects many kinds of stamps; we don't know the specific kind.)

> *My grandfather gives* **advice** *that is not relevant today.*

(He gives many types of irrelevant advice. The type of advice is not specified.)

2. Many proper nouns use no article. Do not use an article with a proper noun unless it is part of the name.

> *The restaurant is on* **Brookhurst Avenue** *near* **Adams Boulevard**.

not

> *The restaurant is on the Brookhurst Avenue near the Adams Boulevard.*

but

> *They had lived in* **the United States** *for six years before they moved to* **the Philippines**. (*The* is part of both names.)

3. Some idiomatic expressions use no article.

> *We love to* **go downtown** *whenever possible.*

> *Do you* **go to school** *every day?*

> *My father* **goes to work** *at 7:30* A.M. *and* **goes to bed** *at 10:00* P.M.

> *Business people always travel* **by plane/bus/train/car**.

> *I spend a lot of time* **at college/home/work**.

Summary of Article Usage

Use the diagram to help you decide which articles to use with nouns.

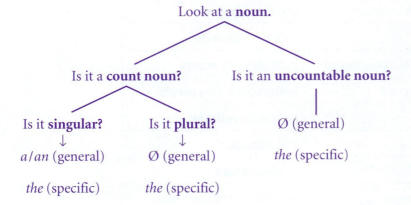

Look at a **noun.**

Is it a **count noun?**   Is it an **uncountable noun?**

Is it **singular?**   Is it **plural?**   Ø (general)
↓   ↓
a/an (general)   Ø (general)   *the* (specific)

the (specific)   *the* (specific)

Circle the sentence that uses articles correctly.

1. **(a)** Doctor must continually update his or her medical knowledge.

   (b) A doctor must continually update his or her medical knowledge.

2. **(a)** The computer is the most important invention of the twentieth century.

   (b) Computer is the most important invention of the twentieth century.

3. **(a)** Reading books is one way to learn about the world.

   (b) Reading book is one way to learn about the world.

4. **(a)** I just bought my mother a gift for her birthday, but I left the gift in my car.

   (b) I just bought my mother a gift for her birthday, but I left a gift in my car.

5. **(a)** Some of homework assignments in math are easy.

   (b) Some of the homework assignments in math are easy.

QUANTIFIERS

Some quantifiers are used only with count nouns, others are used only with uncountable nouns, and some are used with both count and uncountable nouns.

Quantifiers Used with Count Nouns

	QUANTIFIER	COUNT NOUN
Singular	another	another **apple**
	each	each **student**
	every	every **day**
	one	one **test**
Plural	a couple of	a couple of **dollars**
	both	both **children**
	one of the/my/your/our/etc.	one of my **teachers**
	each of the	each of the **students**
	every one of the/my/your/our/etc.	every one of the **essays**
	(not) many/too many	(not) many/too many **people**
	many of the	many of the **colleges**
	a few	a few **friends**
	(very) few	(very) few **books**
	several/a number of	several/a number of **classes**
	a large number of	a large number of **cars**
	two/three	two/three **days**

The number of graduates has ~~ved~~. ⟵ [handwritten note pointing to "several/a number of" and "a large number of" rows]

Quantifiers Used with Uncountable Nouns

QUANTIFIER	UNCOUNTABLE NOUN
a little	a little **salt**
(very) little	(very) little **traffic**
(not) much	(not) much **time**
too much	too much **water**
a great deal of	a great deal of **love**
a large amount of	a large amount of **rain**
a bit of	a bit of **sugar**

Quantifiers Used with Count and Uncountable Nouns

QUANTIFIER	COUNT NOUN	UNCOUNTABLE NOUN
all	all **students**	all **knowledge**
a lot of	a lot of **books**	a lot of **progress**
lots of	lots of **trees**	lots of **patience**
some	some **days**	some **fog**
any	any **magazines**	any **luck**
most	most **workers**	most **advice**
no	no **men**	no **information**
plenty of	plenty of **hypotheses**	plenty of **research**
(the) other	(the) other **assignments**	(the) other **luggage**

NOTE: There is a difference between *few* and *a few* and *little* and *a little*. *A few* means several and expresses a positive meaning. *Few* means almost none. *A little* means some and expresses a positive meaning. *Little* means almost none or not enough.

> *We still have **a few opportunities** to improve our grades.*

(There is still a good chance to improve our grades.)

> *We have **few opportunities** to improve our grades.*

(There isn't much chance to improve our grades.)

> *Raymond's parents give him **a little money** for his tuition.*

(They give him some, or a small amount of, money.)

> *Raymond's parents give him **little money** for his tuition.*

(They don't give him very much money.)

Units of Measure Used with Uncountable Nouns

Units of measure are used with uncountable nouns. The units are countable.

a piece *of candy*	**two pieces** *of candy*
a glass *of milk*	**two glasses** *of milk*
an ounce *of water*	**eight ounces** *of water*
a gallon *of gas*	**ten gallons** *of gas*
a pair *of pants*	**two pairs** *of pants*
Did you put **gas** *in the car?*	*Yes, I bought* **fifteen gallons** *of gas.*
Brice loves **chocolate**.	*In fact, he just ate* **four pieces** *of chocolate.*

Self Check 3

Circle the sentence that uses quantifiers correctly.

1. **(a)** Parents love and protect their children in every cultures.

   (b) Parents love and protect their children in every culture.

2. **(a)** The professor gave us few information about tomorrow's exam.

   (b) The professor gave us little information about tomorrow's exam.

3. **(a)** Andre is very popular at school, but he invited only a few friends to his party.

   (b) Andre is very popular at school, but he invited only a little friends to his party.

4. **(a)** The recipe calls for six ounces of milk.

   (b) The recipe calls for six ounce of milk.

5. **(a)** Our professor gave us too much essays to write this semester.

   (b) Our professor gave us too many essays to write this semester.

DEMONSTRATIVE AND POSSESSIVE ADJECTIVES

Demonstrative Adjectives

1. The demonstrative adjectives are *this, that, these,* and *those. This* and *that* are used with singular count nouns or uncountable nouns, and *these* and *those* are used with plural nouns.

   This house *has three bedrooms.*

   That vocabulary *is very difficult to remember.*

   Let's return **those books** *to the library.*

2. Demonstrative adjectives show the contrast between near and far. *This* and *these* refer to people, objects, or concepts that are close by or that were recently discussed, while *that* and *those* refer to people, objects, or concepts that are at some distance or that were discussed in the past.

> *I took analytic geometry last year.* **That class** *was the hardest one I have ever taken.*

(The class was taken a year ago, so *that* is used to indicate the class's distance from the present.)

> *I didn't understand yesterday's lecture, and* **these notes** *don't make any sense to me.*

(The notes were taken recently and are possibly in the speaker's hands as he or she speaks. *These* indicates close proximity.)

Possessive Adjectives

1. The possessive adjectives are *my, your, his, her, its, one's, our,* and *their.* They can be used with singular or plural nouns.

> **My room** *is on the fifth floor of the dorm.*

> *The host sat* **his guests** *around the dining room table.*

> *Do you know much about* **their research***?*

NOTE: *Your* shows possession; do not confuse it with *you're,* which is the contraction for *you are.*

> **Your** *report was very interesting.* **You're** *an excellent writer.*

Their shows possession; do not confuse it with *they're,* which is the contraction for *they are,* or *there,* which is used to indicate a place.

> **Their** *children are adorable, but* **they're** *very mischievous.* **They're** *playing over* **there.**

Its shows possession; do not confuse it with *it's,* which is the contraction for *it is.*

> *An infant depends on* **its** *parents for everything.* **It's** *impossible for an infant to survive for long on* **its** *own.*

2. *One* means any person or people in general. The use of *one* and the possessive *one's* is impersonal and very formal. It is more common to use the impersonal *you* and *your.*

> *One should take care of* **one's** *health.*

> *You should take care of* **your** *health.* (more common)

NOTE: *One's* shows possession; it is not the contraction for *one is.*

> *It is important to pay attention to* **one's** *diet.*

WRITING TIP

Underline all the singular count nouns in your writing. Make sure that each one is preceded by a determiner.

Circle the sentence that uses demonstrative and possessive adjectives correctly.

1. (a) These grammar is easier for Carlo than for me.

   (b) This grammar is easier for Carlo than for me.

2. (a) Investment counselors recommend learning about your retirement options early.

   (b) Investment counselors recommend learning about you're retirement options early.

3. (a) Where is there new house?

   (b) Where is their new house?

4. (a) Do you remember the movie that we saw last year? That movie had the best action scenes.

   (b) Do you remember the movie that we saw last year? This movie had the best action scenes.

5. (a) Juanita bought this computer programming books over the Internet.

   (b) Juanita bought these computer programming books over the Internet.

EDITING PRACTICE

1. *Put a check (✓) next to the sentences that use nouns and determiners correctly. Correct the sentences that have errors. Correct the verbs if necessary.*

____ **1.** Discriminations against a minority group is illegal.

____ **2.** It is helpful to have good dictionary.

____ **3.** Sebastian got some new clothing. He bought three shirts, two belts, and a pair of pants.

____ **4.** The telephone was an important invention in the late 1800s.

____ **5.** Do you want to study? Let's go to library.

____ **6.** Claudia just moved to a new town, but she already has few friends.

____ **7.** I don't have any money. Do you have a little dollars I can borrow?

____ **8.** One of my favorite dessert is coconut ice cream.

____ **9.** Our high school has smartest academic decathlon team in the state.

____ **10.** All weather reports forecast snow for tomorrow.

____ **11.** Helene has three roommates, and each one has a different schedule.

____ **12.** The first witness during the trial told a lie. Because of a lie, he has to pay

a fine.

____ **13.** The dolphins are considered an intelligent animal.

____ **14.** Authors express their ideas through words.

____ **15.** Do you like this chips from the neighborhood tortillaria?

2. *Complete the following paragraph with the correct nouns and determiners.*

When my teacher asked me to think about _____
                                                        1. a / the
truth behind _____ phrase, "Friends are like family," I
                    2. that / the
recalled the important role that _____ best friend Pierre
                                          3. my / Ø
played in my life during high school. I was a sophomore in high school when

my parents decided to move back to _____ Indonesia. At
                                              4. the / Ø
that point, I had been in _____ United States for six years,
                                5. the / Ø
and I felt that it was more of a home to me than Indonesia. Fortunately,

Pierre and his family agreed to let me live with them until I finished

_____ high school and went off to _____
        6. the / Ø   **7. a / Ø**
college. Pierre and I had been good friends since junior high school when

he moved here from France. We shared _____ similar life
                                                8. much / many
experiences since we were both immigrants in a new country, but it wasn't

until my family moved and I lived with Pierre that I truly understood the

phrase, "Friends are like family." Every _____ of support
                                                  9. type / types
that a family usually provides was provided by my best friend and his

family. Nothing can ever replace the importance of family, but I found that

_____ friends can be a very good substitute and sometimes
        10. Ø / the
even better than the real thing.

3. *In the following paragraph, the underlined determiners and nouns are not correct. Write the correct determiner or noun above each underlined word or phrase.*

Nowadays we frequently hear statements such as "He is like family to me" and "She's just like my sister." Those statements
1
imply the closeness of family but also suggest substituting
friend for family. Are our friends taking place of our families?
2   3
The answer to these question may be found if we look at
4
different age groups. Family and friends have different
importances as we progress through each stages of life. Family
5   6
holds the primary place of influence during childhood, but as
children reach the adolescence, friends begin to take the place
7
of family, and teenagers are likely to feel closer to there friends
8
than to their family. This might remain true until people have
children of their own or they reach old age. At these stages in life, no one can
replace family, and the cycle begins again for children. Furthermore, it is true
that because of the pace and mobility of today's society, friends are taking on
more of tasks once reserved for family members. Hopefully, friends add to the
9
depth and variety of our relationships, but they never replace the important
role that family has played in people's lives throughout histories.
10

4. *The following paragraph has ten errors in the use of nouns or determiners. Find and correct the errors.*

One of the best aspect of my college campus is its diversity. The faculty,

staff, and student come from all over the world. In fact, the professors' and

students' race, economic status, and gender are considered when they are

recruited. Over the past few years, the science department has actively sought female faculty, and this has increased the number of female students in department. Another ways the campus encourages and promotes diversities is through the classes it offers. The humanities and social science departments have several classes that educate students about a variety of cultures, religions, and literatures. These classes are some of most popular on campus and fill up quickly each semesters. As on all college campuses, there are a lot of clubs and student organizations at my school. These social groups encourage students from different backgrounds to mix and get to know each other at informal and friendly gathering. A few groups have cultural nights when their members present songs, dances, and food from different parts of the world. My friends and I especially enjoy tasting food from different regions. I believe that as globalization continues, the steps that my college campus is taking to promote diversity will help it's students understand and accept each other. Hopefully, these simple steps will make the world more peaceful place in the future.

WRITING TOPICS

Study how the student paragraph on page 44 uses count and uncountable nouns and determiners. Circle one example of each kind of determiner studied in this chapter: indefinite and definite articles, ø article, quantifiers, and demonstrative and possessive adjectives. Discuss with a partner why the writer chose each different type of determiner.

Most academic paragraphs, whether they are part of an essay or stand alone, include a clear topic sentence, a body, and a concluding sentence. Notice that this paragraph has these three important parts of an academic paragraph. Use this paragraph as a model when you write about one of the topics on page 44.

The microwave oven is an invention that has changed the world in the last thirty years. Like electricity, the car, and the telephone, the microwave oven has made life easier. Before the microwave, people used only conventional electricity and gas for cooking, but as more women were going to work in the 1970s, the microwave oven let them cook more quickly. The microwave also led to the invention of several new kinds of food such as microwave popcorn and other snacks that children could safely cook by themselves. The microwave has also changed the look of kitchens since all homeowners need a spot for the microwave in their kitchen. It has also increased speed in the fast-food industry. Furthermore, food packaging changed because of the microwave. Due to these changes, the microwave has affected many aspects of life. It's now hard to imagine a world without microwave ovens.

Choose one of the topics below and write at least one paragraph. Use a variety of nouns and determiners. After you complete your first draft, concentrate on editing your work. Keep in mind the editing practice from this chapter.

1. People generally consider telling lies or concealing the truth to be unethical or wrong. However, most people do not tell the complete truth in all situations. Do you believe that deception is ever justified? If so, when do you believe that it is acceptable to tell a lie or to hide the truth? Include examples to support your opinion.

2. The telephone, the car, and the computer are just a few inventions that have significantly changed people's lives. Choose an important invention and describe how life was different before the invention and how life has changed due to this invention.

Go to page 144 for more practice with nouns and determiners.

The Passive Voice

GRAMMAR FOCUS

While the active voice is most common in English, it is important to be able to form and use the passive voice correctly in your writing. The next sections will help you form passive sentences and make decisions on whether to use the passive or active voice.

Notice how the following two sentences have basically the same meaning, but sentence A uses the active voice to focus on the teacher, while sentence B uses the passive voice to focus on the exams.

*(A) The teacher **returned** the exams on Monday.*

*(B) The exams **were returned** on Monday.*

Pretest

Check your understanding of the passive voice. Put a check (✓) next to the sentences that are correct.

_____ **1.** My favorite novel is translate from Russian.

_____ **2.** The photograph will be taken right before sunset.

_____ **3.** More cars were manufactured last year than had been manufactured the year before.

_____ **4.** The package should be send to his business.

_____ **5.** Last year the class teaches by my favorite professor in the department.

_____ **6.** He deserved to be rewarded for his hard work.

_____ **7.** New computer technology is been developed constantly.

_____ **8.** All the exams have been returned.

_____ **9.** The conference was been held at the hotel near the airport.

_____ **10.** Rainbows are always occurred right after rain storms.

Notice how the following paragraph uses both the active and passive voice. Circle the verbs in the passive voice.

A counterfeit product is an imitation that is made so that it looks like the real thing. The counterfeiting of money has been done since money was first used. The counterfeiting that we frequently hear about today involves counterfeit designer products, which are commonly called knockoffs. Some of the most popular knockoffs are handbags, watches, sportswear, and athletic shoes. These are produced and sold to consumers who do not want to pay designer prices but want to own designer goods even though these goods are illegal. Billions of dollars are lost worldwide every year because of counterfeiting. Therefore, governments, retailers, and manufacturers are attempting to stop the manufacture and sale of imitation products.

FORMING THE PASSIVE VOICE

1. The passive voice is formed with the verb *be* + past participle. In the passive voice, the form of *be* indicates the tense. The verb *be* must agree with the subject.

	PRESENT	
Simple Present	*am/is/are* + past participle	The newsletter **is distributed** worldwide.
Present Progressive	*am/is/are being* + past participle	A new library **is being built**.
Present Perfect	*has/have been* + past participle	The house **has been painted** recently.
	PAST	
Simple Past	*was/were* past participle	The library books **were returned** on time.
Past Progressive	*was/were being* + past participle	When I got to the store, the door **was being locked**.
Past Perfect	*had been* + past participle	The dinner **had been prepared** before we arrived.

	FUTURE	
Simple Future	*will be* + past participle	We **will be tested** on this material in two weeks.
Be going to	*am/is/are going to be* + past participle	The show **is going to be held** next month.
Future Perfect	*will have been* + past participle	We **will have been given** the registration materials by then.

NOTE: The present perfect progressive, past perfect progressive, future progressive, and future perfect progressive are very rarely used in the passive voice.

WRITING TIP

In the passive voice, the time frame is indicated by the form of *be*, not the –*ed* ending of the past participle.

present = *All passports* **are** *checked at the airport.*

past = *My passport* **was** *checked an hour ago.*

2. The passive voice can be formed with modals in the present/future and the past.

	MODALS	
Present/Future Modals	**modal** + *be* + **past participle**	The computer **can be upgraded**.
Past Time Modals	**modal** + *have been* + **past participle**	The traffic delays **could have been caused** by the snow.

3. The passive voice can be formed with infinitives and gerunds.

	INFINITIVES AND GERUNDS	
Verbs + Infinitives	**verb** + *to be* + **past participle**	The teacher **likes to be informed** of absences in advance.
Verbs + Gerunds	**verb** + *being* + **past participle**	Oscar **dislikes being treated** like a child.

NOTE: In passive sentences with adverbs of time or frequency, the adverb usually follows *be, have,* or the modal.

The theater **is still being built**.

The parade **has always been held** *on Thanksgiving.*

This door **should never be locked**.

The verb *be* is followed by the present participle to form the present and past progressive in the active voice. The verb *be* is followed by the past participle to form the present and past progressive in the passive voice. Make sure you use the correct participle, present or past, following the verb *be*.

	ACTIVE VOICE	PASSIVE VOICE
Present Progressive	They **are publishing** that book next month. not They are published that book next month.	That book **is being published** next month. not That book is publishing next month.
Past Progressive	They **were preparing** dinner when we arrived. not They were prepared dinner when we arrived.	Dinner **was being prepared** when we arrived. not Dinner was preparing when we arrived.

USING THE PASSIVE VOICE

1. Use the passive voice:

- when the person or thing doing the action (the agent) is obvious, unknown, or unimportant.

  Many trees **were planted** *to replace those lost in the fire.*

  (The focus is on why the trees were planted. Who planted the trees is unknown or unimportant.)

  The house **was built** *in 1860.*

  (The focus is on when the house was built, not on who built it.)

  Tobacco **is grown** *in the South.*

  (The focus is on where tobacco is grown, not by whom.)

- when you don't want to mention the person doing the action.

  Several failing grades **will be received** *at the end of the semester.*

  The information **had been given** *to the media before it was released to the public.*

  The new law **was passed** *without our knowledge.*

- when you want to emphasize the receiver of the action or the result of the action.

  International students **are housed** *with local families when they come to study for short periods of time.*

  A new telephone system that should increase our sales volume **is being installed**.

  Good manners **can be taught** *to children when they are very young.*

- when you are describing a process.

*After the specimens **were collected** and **placed** on the slides, the slides **were observed** under the microscope.*

*The eggs **are beaten** until they are creamy, and then the sugar and butter **are added**.*

*The wheel **must be attached** to the axle before the nuts **are tightened** and the hubcap **is attached**.*

NOTE: The doer of the action may or may not be mentioned in the passive voice. If the person who performed an action is known, the active voice is usually used. However, sometimes when the writer knows who performed the action, he or she will use the passive with the *by* phrase in order to focus on the receiver or result of the action. In the following sentence, the focus is on the two papers, not the writers of the papers.

*The A paper **was written by an undergraduate student**, but the C paper **was written by a graduate student**.*

2. Only transitive verbs (verbs that have a direct object) may be used in the passive voice. Intransitive verbs (verbs that cannot have a direct object) cannot be passive. The following is a list of some commonly used intransitive verbs. Do not use these verbs in the passive voice.

appear	belong	exist	rise
arrive	come	happen	seem
be	die	occur	sleep

*The car accident **happened** at the corner of Sixth Avenue and Main Street.*

not

The car accident was happened at the corner of Sixth Avenue and Main Street.

> **WRITING TIP**
>
> Use a dictionary to check if a verb is transitive or intransitive before using it in the passive voice. At the same time, check its past participle form.

3. Sentences often contain past participle adjectives that look like passive verbs. In these sentences, however, no action is taking place. The adjectives describe an existing situation or state.

*Kendall is **concerned** about her grade in the class.*

*Dat and Amir are **worried** that they may miss their flight.*

*We are **involved** in the International Student Organization.*

> **WRITING TIP**
>
> In spoken English, it is common to use the verb *get* to form the passive voice; however, this is considered informal, and it is generally preferable to use the verb *be* in written English. Edit for the overuse of the verb *get* in your writing.
>
> Preferred   *His first research project **was** published last week.*
>
> Informal   *His first research project **got** published last week.*

Circle the sentence that uses the passive voice correctly.

1. **(a)** I was transferred to the highest group in our math class.

   (b) I was transfer to the highest group in our math class.

2. **(a)** The first reptiles existed during the Paleozoic Era.

   (b) The first reptiles were existed during the Paleozoic Era.

3. **(a)** Many new books are written each year.

   (b) Many new books are writing each year.

4. **(a)** The award will be gave at the ceremony tonight.

   (b) The award will be given at the ceremony tonight.

5. **(a)** I hope to accept at this university.

   (b) I hope to be accepted at this university.

EDITING PRACTICE

1. *Put a check (✓) next to the sentences that use the passive or active voice correctly. Correct the sentences that have errors.*

____ **1.** We think that the research will be finished next year.

____ **2.** Always a meal is served after the lecture.

____ **3.** Children need to be taking care of by their parents.

____ **4.** She is belonged to the academic fraternity on campus.

____ **5.** The fire was put out very quickly.

____ **6.** Most crimes are commit in urban areas.

____ **7.** It is assumed that the senator will resign soon.

____ **8.** At my birthday party, the candles were blew out by my little brother.

____ **9.** The number of graduates has been risen each year.

____ **10.** Before the government banned the pesticide DDT, cancer had been

   linked to its use often.

____ **11.** We denied being given the exam before the test day.

____ **12.** Security measures must develop to prevent more spying.

2. *In the following paragraph, the underlined verbs are not correct. Write the correct verb form above each underlined verb.*

The Olympic Games <u>are believe</u> to be one of the most important athletic
        1

events in the world. They <u>are also seeing</u> as economically, politically, and
        2

socially important for the host city. The Games <u>are seeked</u> by countless
        3

nations so that the host city and country <u>can present</u> to the world in a
        4

positive light. Cities such as Sydney, Barcelona, Beijing, and Vancouver

<u>still remembered</u> for the wonderful events they put on during the two weeks
        5

that the Olympic Games <u>held</u> in those cities. On the other hand, cities that
        6

do a poor job of hosting the Olympics <u>are not allow</u> to forget it. Some
        7

Olympic Games <u>will be remember</u> for tragic events that <u>were happened</u>
        8   9

there, such as the Munich games in 1972 and the Atlanta games in 1996. For

the most part, however, the Games have been a time of peace, friendship,

and hope for both athletes and spectators. It is hoped that these positive

aspects of the Games will continue into the future and that the tragedies

<u>are understood and not forgot</u>.
        10

3. *Complete the following paragraph with the active or passive form of each verb given. Use the time markers to help you choose the best verb tense.*

It is important to remember meaningful events by placing landmarks,

memorials, or statues where these events _____. After WWI
1. occur

and WWII, many statues _____ in cities around the world
2. build

so that we would not forget the wars and the sacrifices that people made

during them. Places of natural beauty are marked in a similar way. National

parks _____ in the United States for the first time in 1912
3. create

to point out the unique beauty of these spots. Since that time, many scenic

places around the world _____ as
4. designate

permanent spots of natural beauty. This means that

in the future these areas _____
5. cannot, develop

and will remain in their natural state. It is also

important to remember events that may not have

worldwide significance but hold community

importance. For example, an event that

_____ a number of years ago in
6. happen

one small community _____.
7. should, remember

A bus full of young children was traveling on a

rural road when it _____ from
8. hit

behind by a large truck. Sadly, several children who were sitting in the rear of

the bus _____, and many more _____
9. kill   **10. injure**

in this accident. Even though the tragedy _____ to be
11. seem

an accident, the community still needs to remember the victims. A tree or

a garden _____ as a living memorial to these children.
12. could, plant

By memorializing significant events and places, people begin to heal their sadness and appreciate the beauty in the world.

4. *The following paragraph has ten errors in the use of the passive voice. Find and correct the errors.*

Watching television still seems to be the most popular leisure activity for many students. Even in the age of the Internet, computer games, and other interactive media, students consistently mention watching television as the way they like to relax. After conducting my informal survey, I was both surprised and pleased by the results. I thought that searching the Internet would be give as the most popular free-time activity; however, I was wrong. Watching television listed as the most popular leisure activity. Although many of the programs on TV are low quality, the television shows that students watch are generally of high quality. Soap operas and "trash" TV were appeared on some students' lists of favorite shows, but the majority listed educational programs. Some differences found between male and female TV viewers. The shows that are watch by males tend to be sports competitions and scientific programming. The programs that are preferring by females are the interview shows and historical documentaries. Both male and female students agreed that political and news shows do not hold their interest. I thought a student's nationality might influence his or her program choices, but program preferences not influenced by this. Even though those who were surveyed are belonged to different gender, age, and nationality groups, television viewing habits were find to be very similar. It is important to note, however, that this survey included only university students, which may have been affected the results.

WRITING TOPICS

Study how this student paragraph uses the passive and active voice. Circle the verbs in the passive voice and underline those in the active voice.

Most academic paragraphs, whether they are part of an essay or stand alone, include a clear topic sentence, a body, and a concluding sentence. Notice that this paragraph has these three important parts of an academic paragraph. Use this paragraph as a model when you write about one of the topics below.

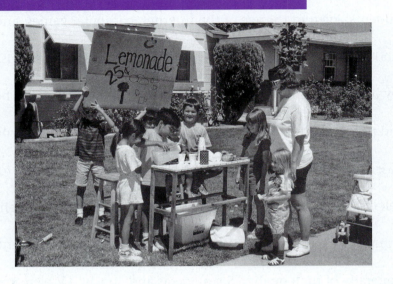

One of my favorite activities as a child was making lemonade. I loved making lemonade because it was a sign of summertime, and I also made some money by selling it. First, the lemons had to be picked from our tree in the backyard. Next, I washed the lemons, and they were cut in half by my mother or older sister. We squeezed the lemons by hand and removed the seeds from the juice. Water and a lot of sugar were boiled together to dissolve the sugar into syrup that was added to the sour lemon juice. Once we had the correct flavor, the lemonade booth was ready to be set up. This was usually near the street in front of my house where the booth could be seen by everyone in the neighborhood. The lemonade was popular with adults and children, and every summer I made a lot of money, but the most important part was the fun that I had in the process.

Choose one of the topics below and write at least one paragraph. Be sure to use the passive voice. After you complete your first draft, concentrate on editing your work. Keep in mind the editing practice from this chapter.

1. Pick a process such as telling a good story, making a cake, or fixing a car and explain how to do it well. What steps should be followed? How much time is needed to complete the process? Where is the process done? Be sure to tell what you like or dislike about this process.

2. Select a recent or historical event from any place around the world. Where did the event occur? How was the world affected by this event? How was this event viewed by the people closest to it and by others around the world? Explain the significance this event has for you and for other people.

Go to page 146 for more practice with the passive voice.

Word Forms and Commonly Confused Words

GRAMMAR FOCUS

Words belong to different parts of speech such as nouns, verbs, and adjectives and can change form according to their part of speech. It is possible to use the correct word in a sentence but the incorrect word form. In this chapter, you will have the opportunity to learn about some common word forms and how they are used in sentences. To begin, consider the related word forms in the following sentences:

VERB	Reading **has strengthened** Jeong's vocabulary.
NOUN	Politics is one of Jeong's **strengths.**
ADJECTIVE	Jeong is a **strong** public speaker.
ADVERB	Jeong spoke **strongly** in favor of the new president.

Pretest

Check your understanding of word forms. Put a check (✓) next to the sentences that are correct.

_____ **1.** E-mail is one of the fastest forms of communication.

_____ **2.** The movie was so scared.

_____ **3.** My best friend finished the work very quick.

_____ **4.** Right now Dan is the worst swimmer in the class, but he tries the hardest.

_____ **5.** We past many large animals along the road in northern Canada.

_____ **6.** Greg is the most fast reader in the class.

_____ **7.** The class was pleased with the high test scores.

_____ **8.** I finished the entirely book in one night.

_____ **9.** You have to get permissioned to use the color copier in the library.

_____ **10.** Erica and Ray are working harder than they worked last year.

Notice the word forms of the underlined words in following paragraph. Label the word form (noun, verb, adjective, adverb) of each underlined word.

Learning a new language can be one of the <u>hardest</u> tasks for an adult, but it's not impossible. Although children learn languages more <u>easily</u> than adults, adults can be <u>successful</u> if they are dedicated. Personality is an important part of language learning. Extroverts can learn languages quicker than introverts because they <u>naturally</u> speak a lot. One of the <u>worst</u> factors for language learning is a high level of anxiety. If someone <u>feels</u> comfortable, he or she is more likely to communicate in a new language. Besides an outgoing <u>personality</u> and a low level of anxiety, high levels of <u>motivation</u> improve one's language

learning. When a person has important reasons to learn a language, it makes the process <u>easier</u>. Various factors work together to make learning a new language easy or difficult, but learners must <u>remember</u> that it can be done with a lot of hard work.

SUFFIXES

The suffix, or ending, of a word can help you recognize its part of speech. For example, *-ent* is an adjective suffix, and *-ence* is a noun suffix.

*Joon is an intellig**ent** student.*

> not

Joon is an intelligence student.

*Independ**ence** is an important American value.*

> not

Independent is an important American value.

WRITING TIP

In addition to the lists on the next page, use a dictionary if you are unsure of suffixes. Many dictionaries include suffixes, indicating their part of speech and their general meaning.

Verb Suffixes

Common verb suffixes include:

-ate	investig**ate**
-en	broad**en**
-ify	not**ify**
-ize	hospital**ize**

Noun Suffixes

Common noun suffixes include:

-ance	toler**ance**		-ist	social**ist**
-cy	accura**cy**		-ity	possibil**ity**
-ence	differ**ence**		-ment	involve**ment**
-er	writ**er**		-ness	happi**ness**
-ion	permiss**ion**		-or	act**or**
-ism	commun**ism**		-ship	friend**ship**

Adverb Suffix

One common adverb suffix is:

-ly	happ**ily**

Adjective Suffixes

Common adjective suffixes include:

-able	accept**able**		-ic	allerg**ic**
-al	classic**al**		-ing	bor**ing**
-an/-ian	Afric**an**, Florid**ian**		-ish	fool**ish**
-ant	toler**ant**		-ive	creat**ive**
-ate	liter**ate**		-less	care**less**
-ed	excit**ed**		-like	child**like**
-ent	depend**ent**		-ly	friend**ly**
-ese	Chin**ese**		-ous	fam**ous**
-ful	help**ful**		-some	hand**some**
-ible	respons**ible**		-y	scar**y**

NOTE: The adjective suffix *-ing* means "causing a feeling." The adjective suffix *-ed* means "experiencing a feeling." For example, an *exciting* person causes a feeling of excitement in other people; an *excited* person feels excitement. The *-ed* adjectives are often used to describe people, whereas the *-ing* adjectives are often used to describe things and actions as well as people.

He was a **boring teacher**, so there were many **bored students** in his class.

At the end of the **tiring day**, the **tired children** were happy to go home.

Self Check 1

Circle the sentence that uses the correct suffix.

1. **(a)** Arab literature is interested to me.

   (b) Arab literature is interesting to me.

2. **(a)** Read the chapter careful.

   (b) Read the chapter carefully.

3. **(a)** Is she a successful businesswoman?

   (b) Is she a success businesswoman?

4. **(a)** I am disappoint about my math grade.

   (b) I am disappointed about my math grade.

5. **(a)** Check in the back of the book for a reference.

   (b) Check in the back of the book for a referencing.

COMPARATIVES AND SUPERLATIVES

Comparatives of Adjectives and Adverbs

Use comparatives when you are looking at the similarities between two related things.

1. Add the comparative suffix *-er* to one-syllable adjectives and adverbs. Since *-er* means "more (than)," do not use *more* with a word that has an *-er* suffix.

   *Marvin is **busier** than I am.* (adjective)

   > not

   Marvin is more busier than I am.

   *Ali works **harder** than Tim.* (adverb)

   > not

   Ali works more harder than Tim.

2. For most adjectives and adverbs with two syllables or more, use *more* for comparatives.

   *I am serious at work, but Marvin is **more serious**.* (adjective)

   *I work carefully, but he works **more carefully**.* (adverb)

3. Use *less* with all adjectives and adverbs when making comparisons that show a smaller amount or a lesser degree.

> I'm **less busy** than Marvin (is).

> I work **less carefully** than Marvin (does).

4. Some adjectives and adverbs have irregular comparative forms.

Better is the comparative form of the adjective *good* and the adverb *well*.

> Jose is a good dancer.   Jose is a **better** dancer than Lee. (adjective)

> Marie sings well.   Marie sings **better** than Paula. (adverb)

Worse is the comparative form of the adjective *bad* and the adverb *badly*.

> My spelling is bad.   My spelling is **worse** than yours. (adjective)

> Martin drives badly.   Martin drives **worse** than Chris. (adverb)

WRITING TIP

Be careful! *Good* is an adjective, and *well* is an adverb. Do not use *good* as an adverb.

*He speaks Italian very **well**.*

     not

He speaks Italian very good.

NOTE: Include *than* if stating the second half of the comparison. It is not always necessary to mention the second half. You may also include the verb or its auxiliary.

> I am **taller than** my sisters (are).

> I walk **faster than** you (do).

Superlatives of Adjectives and Adverbs

Use superlatives when you are comparing three or more things and stating that one of them has the highest degree of the group.

1. Add the superlative suffix *-est* to one-syllable adjectives and adverbs. Include *the* before the superlative. Since *-est* means "the most," do not use *the most* with a word that has an *-est* suffix.

> Alyssa is **the tallest** on her team. (adjective)

>   not

> Alyssa is the most tallest on her team.

> Cathy reads **the fastest** in the class. (adverb)

>   not

> Cathy reads the most fastest in the class.

2. For most adjectives and adverbs with two syllables or more, use *the most*.

> Several stores are convenient, but this one is **the most convenient**.

> I prefer this train to the others, because it runs **the most frequently**.

3. Some adjectives and adverbs have irregular superlative forms.

Best is the superlative form of the adjective *good* and the adverb *well*.

> *Her university has a good education department, but my university has **the best** education department in the state.* (adjective)

> *Adam writes well, but Charlotte writes **the best** in our study group.* (adverb)

Worst is the superlative form of the adjective *bad* and the adverb *badly*.

> *No one in my family is a good singer, and I'm **the worst** of all.* (adjective)

> *Amira performed **the worst** that she has performed all year.* (adverb)

4. Use *the least* with all adjectives and adverbs to show less than anything or anyone else.

> *This is **the least busy** time of the year for the store.* (adjective)

> *This engine runs **the least efficiently** of all the others.* (adverb)

5. The superlative adjective or adverb is often followed by a noun and/or a prepositional phrase, which indicates what is being compared.

> *Angelica is **the most popular** chef.*

> *Joseph works **the hardest** in the class.*

WRITING TIP

Remember: An adjective describes a noun or pronoun and an adverb describes a verb, an adjective, or another adverb.

Self Check 2

Circle the sentence that uses comparatives and superlatives correctly.

1. **(a)** He has the most expensive phone.

   (b) He has the expensivest phone.

2. **(a)** A Honda is more cheaper than a Mercedes-Benz.

   (b) A Honda is cheaper than a Mercedes-Benz.

3. **(a)** We have the baddest record in the tennis league.

   (b) We have the worst record in the tennis league.

4. **(a)** Is the highway more convenient than the side streets?

   (b) Is the highway convenienter than the side streets?

5. **(a)** Abigail did very well on her biology exam.

   (b) Abigail did very good on her biology exam.

COMMONLY CONFUSED WORDS

The following words are often different parts of speech even though they sound similar or the same. By reviewing these word pairs and using a dictionary while you are writing, you will avoid mistakes with these commonly confused words in your writing.

accept	=	verb	*to receive something or give admittance*	Universities only **accept** students for the fall term.
except	=	preposition	*apart from, not included*	We saw the whole movie **except** for the first five minutes.
another	=	noun/pronoun	*an additional*	Josh has a sister in Texas and **another** in Ohio.
	=	adjective/quantifier	*one/one more*	We just finished dessert, but we would like **another** one to take home for our children.
other	=	noun/pronoun	*different from someone/something*	Bo got two As last quarter, one in English and the **other** in psychology.
	=	adjective/quantifier	*additional ones*	Brynn has **other** math problems she still has to solve.
almost	=	adjective (use with *all*)	*not quite all*	We read **almost** all of the book yesterday.
	=	adverb	*nearly*	We **almost** finished the book yesterday.
most/most of	=	adjective/quantifier	*the greatest number or amount*	**Most** students read **most of** the book yesterday.
concern	=	verb	*to worry*	Increasing tuition costs **concern** many students.
be concerned about	=	passive verb phrase	*to be worried about*	Many students **are concerned about** increasing tuition costs.
loss	=	noun	*not winning or no longer having something*	The soccer team has three wins and two **losses.**
lost	=	verb (simple past tense)	*not winning or no longer having something*	I **lost** my credit cards last weekend.
	=	adjective	*not knowing where you are or how to find your way*	The **lost** child is wandering in the mall.

(continued)

past	=	**noun**	the time that existed before the present	My grandmother lives in the **past**.
	=	**adjective**	recent	This **past** year has been difficult.
	=	**preposition**	up to and beyond	He walked **past** me without stopping.
passed	=	**verb (simple past tense)**	succeeded in a test or class	Nicole **passed** the test.
pass	=	**verb (simple present tense)**	succeed in a test or class	I hope we **pass** the final.
wish	=	**verb**	to want something to be true although it's impossible or unlikely	The students **wish** that they had studied more.
hope	=	**verb**	to want something to happen that is possible or likely	The students **hope** that they pass the exam.
beside	=	**preposition**	next to, at the side of	Please put the book **beside** the papers.
besides	=	**preposition/ transition**	in addition to	**Besides** security, dogs provide companionship.
borrow	=	**verb**	to use something temporarily that belongs to someone else	Jason **borrowed** a book from the library to read while he was on vacation.
lend	=	**verb**	to give something temporarily to someone else	My father will **lend** me money, but I have to pay it back with interest.
a number of + plural verb	=	**noun/quantifier**	several, many	A **number of** tourists are arriving today.
the number of + singular verb	=	**noun/quantifier**	the total number	**The number of** tourists is unknown right now.
worse	=	**comparative form of *bad* and *badly***	not as good as	Robin is **worse** than I am at dancing.
worst	=	**superlative form of *bad* and *badly***	the lowest quality of anything else of the same type	Whose score is the **worst**?
like	=	**preposition**	having the same qualities as something else	A violin sounds **like** a viola to me.
	=	**transition**	similar to	**Like** the United Kingdom, Australia has a parliamentary government.
alike	=	**adjective**	very similar	The twins look exactly **alike**.

Circle the sentence that uses the commonly confused word correctly.

1. **(a)** His score is worse on the second test than on the first one.

   (b) His score is worst on the second test than on the first one.

2. **(a)** Always keep your suitcase besides you at the airport.

   (b) Always keep your suitcase beside you at the airport.

3. **(a)** The World Cup loss was sad for the whole country.

   (b) The World Cup lost was sad for the whole country.

4. **(a)** Almost energy produces some pollution.

   (b) Almost all energy produces some pollution.

5. **(a)** We passed the airport on our way home.

   (b) We past the airport on our way home.

WRITING TIP

Use the spell-check tool on your computer before you print your paper. It will help catch general spelling errors. Be careful, however, because it won't always find errors in easily confused words and word forms.

EDITING PRACTICE

1. *Put a check (✓) next to the sentences that use word forms and commonly confused words correctly. Correct the sentences that have errors. If necessary, use a dictionary to check for the correct word form.*

_____ **1.** The United States has a diversity population.

_____ **2.** I feel embarrass when I receive a poor grade on an exam.

_____ **3.** You should notify your teacher if you are going to be absent.

_____ **4.** Which way to downtown is the quickest?

_____ **5.** Responsible is something people learn as they become adults.

_____ **6.** He has a distance relative that is coming to visit next month.

_____ **7.** The computer industry is stronger than the automobile industry in this

country.

_____ **8.** Phong had feelings of happy, doubt, and pain.

_____ **9.** I'm not going to give up time with my family to become more richer.

_____ **10.** She concerns the upcoming exam.

_____ **11.** They work so well together.

_____ **12.** That is the importantest document that I have ever signed.

_____ **13.** Mario must length his essay to meet the page requirement.

_____ **14.** My two brothers look like, but they are not twins.

_____ **15.** A number of small businesses go out of business each year.

2. *In the following paragraphs, the underlined words are not correct. Write the correct word above each underlined error. Use a dictionary if necessary to check for the correct word form.*

The novel *Travels with Charley* describes John Steinbeck's experiences as

he travels from one <u>coastal</u> of the United States to the other. He is traveling
₁

alone <u>accept</u> for a companion named Charley, a big <u>friend</u> dog. We get to
₂ ₃

know Charley <u>good</u> by the end of the novel because the author writes so
₄

much about him. Even though Charley is a lazy dog, he is <u>more smart</u> than
₅

many other dogs. In fact, sometimes Steinbeck is even <u>foolisher</u> than Charley.
₆

Charley also adds <u>excited</u> moments to the story. For example, Charley's
₇

behavior when Steinbeck is stopped by the police is one of the <u>interestingest</u>
₈

parts of the novel.

Although there are many good parts in *Travels with Charley*, I believe the

novel is a little <u>disappointed</u>. I <u>hope</u> the story had more details about life in
₉ ₁₀

the United States than Charley's adventures. For me the <u>pleasantest</u> part of
₁₁

the book is when Steinbeck writes about the North American scenery and

people. However, some people prefer a story about a supportive friendship,

which is the most important theme in *Travels with Charley*. Therefore, I have

already <u>borrowed</u> my book to a friend who wants to read a story with this
₁₂

theme.

3. *Read the following paragraph. Complete the paragraph with the correct form of each word given. If necessary, use a dictionary to select suffixes for different parts of speech.*

The traditional roles that men and women have played

throughout history have been very _____. In many
        1. differ

_____, most jobs and activities are still divided into
   2. cultural

men's or women's work. In _____ cultures or families,
       3. tradition

the women accept the secondary role and are _____ on
          4. depend

men for _____ support and leadership within the family.
   5. finance

In many parts of the world, these roles are changing as women take over

some of the duties that men have _____ held. In many
        6. tradition

cases men _____ hand over their positions of dominance.
    7. glad

In addition, men and women now have equal educational opportunities

and job prospects after their _____ from high school or
      8. graduate

college. It is impossible to say which system is the _____
          9. good

one, but people no longer question a woman's right to pursue a career and

have a family or a man's _____ to make the family his
     10. decide

first priority. These are _____ advances for both sexes and
    11. signify

changes that make life _____ than it was in the past.
    12. easy

4. *The following paragraph has ten errors in the use of word forms and commonly confused words. Find and correct the errors. If necessary, use a dictionary to find the correct word form.*

When I describe myself as a writer, the first word that I think of is *slow*. I have to think about a topic for several days before I begin to write, but the most tough part is still the first few words. Sometimes I sit impatient at the computer for hours and end up without any words on the screen. I know that writing is a slow process, but I am frustrating when I cannot find the right words. Once I am passed the introduction, I can write the body and conclusion rapid. Because of my slow writing speed, in-class essays are worst than out-of-class writing. When I have only a short period of time to complete an essay, the process is very frightened to me. I usually write very slow on these tests and never have time to finish. Even though writing makes me uncomfortable, I understand the important of this skill. I wish I can become a good writer soon by practicing my writing skills more often.

WRITING TOPICS

Study how this student paragraph uses word forms and commonly confused words. Label the word forms of the underlined words. Circle two of the commonly confused pairs of words that you studied in this chapter. Most academic paragraphs, whether they are part of an essay or stand alone, include a clear topic sentence, a body, and a concluding sentence. Notice that this paragraph has these three important parts of an academic paragraph. Use this paragraph as a model when you write about one of the topics below.

Dogs make the best pets because they bring so many <u>different</u> types of joy to their owners. I know that this is true because in the past I had a pet dog that was my best friend. My dog, Mr. Scruff, was my loyal companion for more than ten years. We did everything together. Mr. Scruff <u>walked</u> with me to my first day of school, played with me in the snow and the sun, and slept with me every night for years. Besides being <u>wonderful</u> companions, dogs can teach their owners <u>responsibility</u>. I had to feed, bathe, and care for Mr. Scruff every day. I made sure he didn't get fleas and always had water in his bowl. It was a wonderful feeling to know that Mr. Scruff <u>depended</u> on me for so much. <u>Loyalty</u> is another reason that dogs are the <u>greatest</u> pets. Dogs love their

owners no matter how <u>badly</u> the owners may act. When I started high school, I didn't pay much attention to Mr. Scruff, but he still treated me as his best friend. If I forgot to feed him, he still showed me love. If I didn't play with him after school, he remained at my side. I passed through this phase <u>quickly</u> but learned that dogs show loyalty that humans are not capable of.

The loss of Mr. Scruff was almost <u>sadder</u> than when I lost some people in my life. Like many dogs, he was beside me for both good and bad times. For these reasons and many more, dogs are the most wonderful pets in the world.

Choose one of the topics and write at least one paragraph. After you complete your first draft, concentrate on editing your work. Keep in mind the editing practice from this chapter.

1. Many people believe that in some Western societies or countries, the elderly are not treated well. From your experiences or observations, is this true? Compare how the elderly are treated in two cultures that you are familiar with.

2. People own pets for companionship, protection, and other reasons. Do you have a pet now, did you have one in the past, or do you plan to have one in the future? Why or why not? Which type of animal makes the best pet?

Go to page 148 for more practice with word forms and commonly confused words.

6 Verb Forms, Gerunds, and Infinitives

GRAMMAR FOCUS

There are five basic verb forms in English:

BASE FORM	write
THIRD-PERSON SINGULAR	writes
SIMPLE PAST	wrote
PRESENT PARTICIPLE	writing
PAST PARTICIPLE	written

The first part of this chapter will review the five verb forms that you practiced in earlier chapters. In the following section, gerunds (verb + -ing) and infinitives (to + verb) will be introduced. If the verb form, gerund, or infinitive in a sentence is used correctly, the sentence is accurate and easy to understand. All writers need to edit carefully for these structures.

Notice the use of gerunds and infinitives in the two sentences below. After *finish*, it is necessary to use a gerund, while after *want*, it is necessary to use an infinitive.

> Enrique **finished writing** his essay minutes before it was due.

> He **wanted to finish** it earlier, but he procrastinated all weekend.

Pretest

Check your understanding of verb forms, gerunds, and infinitives. Put a check (✓) next to the sentences that are correct.

_____ **1.** Jun didn't took the driver's test last week.

_____ **2.** I haven't boughten any new clothes recently.

_____ **3.** The teacher let us to use our books on the test.

_____ **4.** Are you interested in going to a golf tournament this weekend?

_____ **5.** They avoid to drive at rush hour.

_____ **6.** Emily loves to read nineteenth-century English literature.

_____ **7.** Please don't make me to practice anymore.

_____ **8.** Johnnie is accustomed to studying late at night.

_____ **9.** Mr. Tang plans to go on a cruise from Mexico to Cuba.

_____ **10.** I miss to see my family.

The following paragraph uses many gerunds and infinitives. Some of them are underlined. Notice the verbs that come before each gerund or infinitive. Complete the exercise below the paragraph by circling the word gerund *or* infinitive.

To be successful at school, good reading skills are necessary. Good readers (1) suggest <u>following</u> a few steps to improve one's reading skills. Before good readers (2) begin <u>reading</u>, they review the article or book. First, they look at the title, the pictures, and all bold words or headings. They (3) hope <u>to find</u> information that is familiar. They say it is important to remember everything you already know about the topic of the article or book. When they (4) finish <u>reviewing</u> the topic, they (5) begin <u>to read</u>. Good readers (6) advise <u>taking</u> notes during the reading process. Short notes in the margin (7) help them <u>to remember</u> important points. Good readers always (8) expect <u>to read</u> the article several times. They (9) keep <u>rereading</u> the article until they are confident about its content. This process is not easy or fast, but good readers (10) don't mind <u>doing</u> it because it contributes to their success.

1. *suggest* + gerund / infinitive

2. *begin* + gerund / infinitive

3. *hope* + gerund / infinitive

4. *finish* + gerund / infinitive

5. *begin* + gerund / infinitive

6. *advise* + gerund / infinitive

7. *help* + gerund / infinitive

8. *expect* + gerund / infinitive

9. *keep* + gerund / infinitive

10. *mind* + gerund / infinitive

THE SIMPLE TENSES

1. In the simple present, use the base form and the third-person singular. Use the auxiliary verb *do* in negatives and questions except with the verb *be*. (See Chapter 1.)

I usually **make** *dinner.*	*He sometimes* **makes** *breakfast.*
John **does not like** *red meat.*	*Where* **do** *they* **eat** *lunch?*
Kate **is** *a vegetarian.*	*They* **are not** *good cooks.*

2. In the simple past, use the simple past form of the verb. Use the auxiliary verb *did* in negatives and questions except with the verb *be*. (See Chapter 1.)

My cousin **visited** me last month.   We **went** to the beach together.

They **did not have** time to see us.   Where **did** Rich and Darla **go**?

Joy **was** at the beach.   We **were not** on time.

NOTE: The auxiliary *do* is always followed by the base form of the verb.

They **did not come**.

              not
They did not came.

THE PROGRESSIVE TENSES

In the present progressive and past progressive, use the auxiliary *be* followed by the present participle of the main verb (*-ing* form). The form of *be* shows present or past time. (See Chapter 1.)

Are you **doing** your homework now? (present progressive)

Last year at this time, Doris **was visiting** friends in Brazil. (past progressive)

THE PERFECT TENSES

In the present perfect and past perfect, use the auxiliary *have* followed by the past participle of the main verb (*-ed, -en,* or *-t* form). The form of *have* shows present or past time. (See Chapter 1.)

Has she **seen** the new museum yet? (present perfect)

The Halloween party **had ended** by midnight. (past perfect)

> **WRITING TIP**
> Remember to check a dictionary to make sure you are using the correct forms for irregular simple past verbs and past participles.

MODALS

1. In the present or future, modals are always followed by the base form of the main verb. (See Chapter 2.)

I **should write** thank-you notes for my birthday gifts.

Can you **come** with us to the play?

2. In the past, modals are generally followed by *have* + past participle. (See Chapter 2.)

The Titanic **should have provided** lifeboats for all passengers.

Circle the sentence that forms verbs correctly.

1. **(a)** Did Barack Obama won the election in 2008?

   (b) Did Barack Obama win the election in 2008?

2. **(a)** Melissa and Carson are not at school today.

   (b) Melissa and Carson don't be at school today.

3. **(a)** The children visiting their grandparents right now.

   (b) The children are visiting their grandparents right now.

4. **(a)** We bought a hybrid car. You buy one too?

   (b) We bought a hybrid car. Did you buy one too?

5. **(a)** She can plays the harmonica very well.

   (b) She can play the harmonica very well.

GERUNDS AND INFINITIVES

In addition to the five basic forms, verbs in English also have a gerund (verb + *-ing*) and an infinitive form (*to* + verb). In these forms, however, the verb no longer acts as a verb. Gerunds and infinitives act as nouns—for example, as subjects or as objects of verbs and prepositions.

Verb + Gerund or Infinitive

Some verbs are followed by either a gerund or an infinitive as their object. An object receives the action of the verb.

> *She **hates swimming/to swim** in the ocean.*
>
> *Our cousins **have loved reading/to read** since they were children.*
>
> *We **preferred studying/to study** at the library last year.*

These verbs include:

begin	continue	hate	like	love	prefer	start

Verb + Gerund

Some verbs are followed by a gerund but not an infinitive as their object.

> *I **avoid working out** at the gym.*
>
> *Aaron **dislikes traveling** by bus.*
>
> *Susan **suggested seeing** the new ballet performance.*

These verbs include:

appreciate	delay	dislike	keep	miss
avoid	deny	enjoy	mention	quit
consider	discuss	finish	mind	suggest

Verb + Infinitive

Some verbs are followed by an infinitive, or a noun or pronoun + infinitive, but not a gerund as their object.

> Susan **agreed to go** to the concert.
>
> The university **requires applicants to write** an essay.
>
> They **invited me to join** them for dinner.

These verbs include:

agree	encourage	intend	offer	pretend	tell
ask	expect	invite	order	remind	want
decide	hope	learn	plan	seem	warn

Adjective + Infinitive

Some adjectives can be followed by infinitives. These kinds of sentences frequently use *it* as the subject of the sentence.

> **It** *is* **difficult to graduate** *from college in four years.*
>
> *The students are* **happy to have** *a long vacation.*

Adjectives that can be followed by infinitives include:

afraid	eager	important	possible/impossible
anxious	easy	likely	proud
dangerous	happy/sad	lucky	right
difficult	hard	necessary/unnecessary	wrong

Preposition + Gerund

1. Prepositions such as *in, on, by, for,* and *with* can be followed by gerunds but not infinitives.

   > He had a good reason **for arriving** late.

2. Phrasal verbs (verbs that consist of two or three words) and other verb + preposition combinations can also be followed by gerunds but not infinitives.

   > *Students often* **put off studying** *until the last minute.*
   >
   > *I* **am accustomed to skipping** *breakfast before school.*
   >
   > **Have** *you* **thought about going** *to graduate school?*

   Common phrasal verbs followed by gerunds include:

apologize for	give up	look forward to	prohibit (someone) from	talk about
believe in	insist on	look into	put off	think about
complain about	keep on	plan on	take care of	

Common *be* + adjective + preposition combinations followed by gerunds include:

be accustomed to	be bored with	be interested in	be tired of
be afraid of	be excited about	be preoccupied with	be worried about

WRITING TIP

Be careful! Do not confuse the preposition *to* (as in *be accustomed to, look forward to,* etc.) with the *to* used in the infinitive (*to go, to be,* etc.). The preposition *to* is followed by a gerund. The infinitive *to* is followed by the base form of the verb.

Verb + Base Form

The verbs *make, have, let,* and *help* can mean to cause someone to do something or to allow someone to do something. When they are used in this way, these verbs are followed by the base form of a verb. *Make, have, let,* and *help* must be followed by a pronoun or noun phrase + the base form of the verb. *Help* can be followed by an infinitive or a base form.

> The coach **made us run** two miles, and he **had us do** sit-ups afterwards.
>
> She **lets her teenage daughter go** on dates.
>
> **Can** you **help me (to) paint** the living room?

Self Check 2

Circle the sentences that use gerunds, infinitives, or base forms correctly.

1. (a) He was eager to move from an apartment to a house.

   (b) He was eager move from an apartment to a house.

2. (a) He hopes to see a Broadway show in New York.

   (b) He hopes seeing a Broadway show in New York.

3. (a) The hike made them felt tired all day

   (b) The hike made them feel tired all day.

4. (a) They are excited about join the club.

   (b) They are excited about joining the club.

5. (a) I look forward to swim this summer.

   (b) I look forward to swimming this summer.

WRITING TIP

Edit your writing on a paper copy rather than on the computer screen. Editing is more thorough and accurate when it is done on paper.

EDITING PRACTICE

1. *Put a check (✓) next to the sentences that use verb forms, gerunds, and infinitives correctly. Correct the sentences that have errors.*

_____ **1.** Counselors advised us to begin our university applications early.

_____ **2.** Bad pet owners let their animals to wander in the streets.

_____ **3.** Mr. Gong made his son study medicine.

_____ **4.** Praise helps children improving their behavior.

_____ **5.** The Berlin Wall doesn't divides East and West Berlin anymore.

_____ **6.** Mrs. Hasam suggested taking a taxi to the party.

_____ **7.** When the wind blowing through the trees, it sounds beautiful.

_____ **8.** The college campus cover 300 acres.

_____ **9.** Has the letter carrier being to your house yet today?

_____ **10.** I apologized for losing Anthony's book.

_____ **11.** Greta didn't found the ring that she lost last week.

_____ **12.** The students look forward to finish the project.

_____ **13.** It is necessary to get eight hours of sleep each night.

2. *In the following paragraph, the underlined verbs are not correct. Write the correct verb form, gerund, or infinitive above each underlined verb phrase.*

Keeping healthy is an

important part of a good life.

Typically, people <u>are live</u> longer

              1

now than in the past. However,

we are not always healthier.

Many people <u>dislike to change</u>

              2

their diet and exercise habits even though the changes <u>may making</u> them feel

                                                  3

better in old age. People <u>do not likes</u> to make changes now for their future.

                        4

Even though most people <u>are worried about lose</u> weight, obesity rates

                             5

continue to rise. If this problem is not controlled, most obese people

<u>will developing</u> many health problems later in life. Because of this, some
    6

people <u>have improve</u> their eating and exercise habits. There are many people
    7

who <u>have decided eating</u> a healthy diet, but others <u>let themselves to become</u>
    8   **9**

lazy about food. If people eat a healthy diet, it makes them <u>enjoy to exercise</u>
    10

more, and a small amount of exercise <u>helps people eating</u> well. Thus, one
    11

good lifestyle change can lead to another. It is interesting that in the past,

people <u>did not worried</u> as much as we do today about living healthy lives, yet
    12

their health was probably better than ours.

3. *Read the following paragraph. Complete the paragraph with the correct form of each verb given.*

In the United States during World War II, many Japanese Americans were

sent to internment camps.[1] These Americans did not _____
    1. understand

why they were treated as criminals; however, the U.S. government believed

that Japanese Americans might _____ the Japanese military
    2. support

during the war. Many of these Japanese Americans were sent to Manzanar,

an internment camp in central California. At Manzanar, camp officials did

not _____ the camp residents _____
    3. help   **4. adapt**

to their new surroundings. The Japanese Americans were alone and could

only _____ for release from the camp. As World War
    5. hope

II was _____, the government let some internees[2]
    6. end

_____ to U.S. locations east of California. After the
    7. move

war had finally _____, Japanese Americans were forced
    8. end

_____ the camps. They began _____
    9. leave   **10. think**

about returning to their old lives. Since World War II, Americans have

---

[1]**internment camps:** areas where prisoners are held, especially during war
[2]**internees:** people in internment camps, prisoners

slowly learned about this part of U.S. history, and many are interested in

_____ to correct this past mistake. Remembering past
      11. try

mistakes may allow us _____ these kinds of actions in the
                                12. avoid

future.

4. *The following paragraph has ten errors in the use of verb forms, gerunds, and infinitives. Find and correct the errors.*

    Los Angeles is a wonderful city. It is sad that the city has receive a bad image because of smog, crime, and gangs. Although the city has some problems, tourists should not to overlook it as a vacation spot. In fact, southern California residents ought to think about visit downtown Los Angeles more often. This area has becomes a center of excitement and diversity. Koreatown, Little Tokyo, and Olvera Street are all close to each other. This racial diversity helps everyone understanding other cultures and beliefs; it also helps them accepting differences more easily. The city's art community is also very good. Previously, Los Angeles did not had a theater district like New York City does, but now there are many large and small theaters throughout the city. Los Angeles has always being famous for Hollywood, and it's still an exciting part of the city. Hollywood is responsible for entertain the world and promises to impressing everyone who goes there. These are only a few of the many reasons that Los Angeles is a great place to vacation and live.

WRITING TOPICS

Study the student paragraph that uses verbs from this chapter. The underlined verbs are followed by gerunds, infinitives, or base verbs. Circle the gerund, infinitive, or base verb that follows each underlined verb.

Most academic paragraphs, whether they are part of an essay or stand alone, include a clear topic sentence, a body, and a concluding sentence. Notice that this paragraph has these three important parts of an academic paragraph. Use this paragraph as a model when you write about one of the topics below.

I <u>am accustomed to</u> studying and working most of the time, but I <u>look forward to</u> relaxing when I have free time. The different ways that I relax are bicycling, reading, and listening to music. I <u>decided</u> to ride my bike to school and work because it <u>helps</u> me relax at the end of the day. Fresh air and exercise are good ways to lower stress. Bicycling offers both of these benefits and <u>makes</u> me relax every afternoon. Besides bicycling, I always <u>insist on</u> reading before I go to bed at night. This activity <u>seems</u> to help me sleep better and feel energetic in the morning. Sometimes instead of reading, I <u>enjoy</u> listening to music in my free time. I <u>am always excited about</u> hearing a new band and talking about music with my friends. Bicycling, reading, and listening to music are free-time activities that are both enjoyable and healthful. I <u>encourage</u> my friends to try these three activities in their free time too. We all need to <u>think about</u> enjoying our free time in relaxing ways.

Choose one of the topics and write at least one paragraph. Use some of the verbs from the lists given in this chapter as well as some of your own. After you complete your first draft, concentrate on editing your work. Keep in mind the editing practice from this chapter.

1. Everyone has different ways of spending his or her free time. Write about one or more ways that you like to spend your leisure time. Think about the following questions as you write. Do you exercise, read, play sports, shop, sleep, or study? How often do you do this activity? Is it an activity that you do alone or with a group? What benefits do you gain by doing this activity?

2. Some people prefer to live in large cities, others prefer the suburbs, and many like the countryside. Which do you prefer and why? These locations are different from one another because of their pace of life, safety, recreation, education, and job opportunities. Some things to think about include: What do you like about the location where you live? What do you dislike about other locations? Where do you live now, and where have you lived in the past? How have these locations helped you develop your preferences?

Go to page 150 for more practice with verb forms, gerunds, and infinitives.

7 Coordination and Parallel Structure

GRAMMAR FOCUS

By using coordination, a writer gives equal importance to two or more ideas within a sentence. Coordinating conjunctions are used to join two or more similar grammatical structures such as words, phrases, or clauses. Different coordinating conjunctions show the relationship between the parts of a sentence. In the following example, notice how the conjunction *but* joins two independent clauses and at the same time shows the contrast between them.

Engineers need excellent math skills, **but** *they need good verbal skills, too.*

Parallel structure means that the words, phrases, or clauses that are joined by coordinating conjunctions are the same grammatical structure. The following example uses the coordinating conjunction *and* to join the three parallel adjectives.

Undergraduate engineering majors must demonstrate their excellent <u>math, verbal,</u> **and** *<u>writing</u> skills during interviews for professional positions.*

This chapter will help you select the appropriate coordinating conjunction for the meaning you wish to convey, place the conjunction within the sentence correctly, and use parallel structure.

Pretest

Check your understanding of coordination and parallel structure. Put a check (✓) next to the sentences that are correct.

_____ **1.** The reading passage discusses the American value of independence, it also points out other common values.

_____ **2.** Racism results in hatred, fear, and unfair.

_____ **3.** The business world provides financial rewards, and people tend to pursue these rather than the emotional rewards of friends and family.

_____ **4.** Simon loves English literature, but he wants to take three English classes next semester.

_____ **5.** Not only smoking damages your lungs, but it also decreases bone density.

_____ **6.** People make promises, yet the promises are not always kept.

_____ **7.** People should eat a lot of beans and grains, for their health benefits are well known.

_____ **8.** Seema cancelled her trip to India she will go next year instead.

_____ **9.** The music industry decreased its sales of CDs, increased its digital sales, and broadened its services in the past decade.

_____ **10.** Hasad neither talks to his parents nor his siblings every day.

The following paragraph uses coordination and parallel structure. Two coordinating conjunctions are underlined. Find two more examples of coordinating conjunctions to underline in the paragraph. Two examples of parallel structure are circled. Find one more example of parallel structure to circle in the paragraph.

Although the most famous amusement park in the world is Disneyland, Disney did not invent the idea of amusement parks. Amusement parks started as temporary fairs or carnivals in Europe, and the first permanent amusement park was built in 1583 in Denmark. In the early 1900s, amusement parks became very popular in the United States because people had more free time and money to spend on leisure activities. Amusement parks were popular through the 1920s, but the Great Depression and World War II caused a decline in their use. Amusement parks became popular again in the 1950s with Disneyland. With their new popularity, modern parks began to offer more than rides. There are movies, television shows, toys, and songs that the parks create. The most successful amusement parks today have evolved into resorts with hotels, restaurants, and sports facilities. Amusement parks have always been an escape from the real world, for they transport us from the violence, litter, and social problems outside their walls.

FORMING SENTENCES WITH COORDINATING AND CORRELATIVE CONJUNCTIONS

FANBOY

1. Coordinating conjunctions include:

and	but	for	nor	or	so	yet

Correlative, or paired, conjunctions include:

both . . . and	either . . . or	neither . . . nor	not only . . . but also

2. Coordinating and correlative conjunctions join:

- words

  Masis **and** *Yuri* fled the war in Armenia.

  The book was **neither** *well written* **nor** *interesting*.

- phrases

  They are proud of their country **but** *not of their president*.

  Both *his books* **and** *his speeches are extremely well written*.

- dependent clauses

  If the children behave **and** *if we have enough time*, *we will stop for ice cream*.

- independent clauses

  They had to leave their country, **for** *there was no future there*.

  Yesterday it **not only** *rained*, **but** *it* **also** *snowed*.

79

3. When two independent clauses are joined with a coordinating or correlative conjunction, a comma goes before the conjunction. No comma is needed when two phrases or words are joined.

Comma	Students can develop job skills at school, **or** the skills can be learned through on-the-job training.
	Not only is James an excellent music teacher, **but** he is also a talented guitar player.
No comma	Computer scientists **and** engineers need strong problem-solving skills.
	Both lunch and dinner will be served at the conference.
	Studying abroad in a European country **or** in an Asian country is a great way to experience another culture.
	Neither the campus bookstore **nor** the downtown bookstore has the book I need.

WRITING TIP

Avoid beginning a sentence with a coordinating conjunction. Because coordinating conjunctions show the relationship between two or more sentence parts, these conjunctions generally appear between sentence parts rather than at the beginning of a sentence.

Preferred: *Election volunteers can mail campaign literature,* **or** *they can telephone registered voters.*

Less formal: *Election volunteers can mail campaign literature.* **Or** *they can telephone registered voters.*

Preferred: *We arrived at the sale late,* **so** *we missed the best deals.*

Less formal: *We arrived at the sale late.* **So** *we missed the best deals.*

4. In sentences with correlative conjunctions, the subject that is closer to the verb determines if the verb is singular or plural.

Not only *my best friend, but* my parents are *also here.*

Not only *my parents, but* my best friend is *also here.*

5. Use coordinating conjunctions as one way to avoid run-on sentences and comma splice errors.

Run-on: *Colin's GPA went down last year he needs to study more this semester to improve it.*

Comma splice: *Colin's GPA went down last year, he needs to study more this semester to improve it.*

Correct sentence: *Colin's GPA went down last year,* **so** *he needs to study more this semester to improve it.*

6. Coordinating conjunctions cannot be combined with other conjunctions within the same sentence.

Incorrect: *Although the club president chose the location for the party, but not all of the members are happy with her decision.*

Incorrect: *Although the club president chose the location for the party, not all of the members are happy with her decision.*

USING COORDINATING AND CORRELATIVE CONJUNCTIONS

1. Each coordinating conjunction has a different use.

COORDINATING CONJUNCTION	USE	EXAMPLE	
and	to add information	Daniela is going downtown to meet a friend **and** to hear a lecture.	
but	to show contrast	The downtown area will be crowded, **but** Daniela really wants to hear the lecture.	
or	to express a choice	Daniela hasn't decided if she is going to drive **or** take the bus.	
yet	to show contrast	Daniela sees her friend frequently, **yet** she still looks forward to meeting her.	
so	to show a result	Daniela still needs to buy tickets to the lecture, **so** she needs to arrive a little early.	
for	to show a reason	Daniela and her friend won't stay out late, **for** they both have to work the next day.	

NOTE: The conjunction *for* means *because*, but it is not used very often to express this meaning. The preferred connector is *because*.

2. Use correlative or paired conjunctions rather than coordinating conjunctions to add emphasis to the parts being joined or to express a choice.

To add emphasis, use *both . . . and* or *not only . . . but also*.

> **Both** solar **and** wind energy are alternatives to oil and coal.

> Computer hackers **not only** damage computer systems **but also** slow business.

To express a choice, use *either . . . or*.

> He wants a computer made by **either** Dell **or** Apple.

To emphasize that two things are negative, use *neither . . . nor*.

> **Neither** newspapers **nor** television news can compete with the Internet.

WRITING TIP

That is not a coordinating conjunction; it cannot be used in the same way as *and, but, so, or, nor, yet,* or *for.*

*The council meeting will be televised, **so** all citizens can watch the debate.*

or

*The council meeting will be televised, **and** all citizens can watch the debate.*

not

The council meeting will be televised, that all citizens can watch the debate.

Circle the sentence that uses coordination correctly.

1. **(a)** We worked all night, so we didn't meet our deadline.

    (b) We worked all night, yet we didn't meet our deadline.

2. **(a)** I drank the coffee, it was bitter.

    (b) I drank the coffee, but it was bitter.

3. **(a)** Their study group worked hard, so they finished the project early.

    (b) Their study group worked hard, that they finished the project early.

4. **(a)** The lake was closed due to contamination but people were still walking along the shoreline.

    (b) The lake was closed due to contamination, but people were still walking along the shoreline.

5. **(a)** Neither my sister nor <u>my parents are</u> here.

    (b) Neither my sister nor my parents is here.

PARALLEL STRUCTURE

1. When you join words, phrases, or clauses with coordinating conjunctions, they must be parallel. That is, they must be the same grammatical structure.

> *<u>Russian cosmonauts,</u> <u>American astronauts,</u> **and** <u>private citizens</u> are now traveling to the International Space Station.* (nouns)

> *They <u>are finishing</u> their experiments **and** <u>(are) leaving</u> for home soon.* (verbs)

> *Their experiments in space are <u>expensive</u> **but** <u>important</u> for advancing our knowledge.* (adjectives)

> *The astronauts try <u>to ride</u> a stationary bicycle **or** <u>to run</u> on a treadmill every day while they are in space.* (infinitives)

> *<u>Working,</u> <u>eating,</u> **and** <u>sleeping</u> in such a small space requires cooperation.* (gerunds)

> *The results of their experiments will be used <u>in many industries,</u> <u>with surprising applications,</u> **and** <u>for years to come</u>.* (prepositional phrases)

> *<u>Astronauts train for possible emergencies at the Space Station,</u> **but** <u>they have never had to use this training</u>.* (independent clauses)

NOTE: When you write a sentence that includes more than two parallel items, use commas to separate them. The comma before the conjunction is optional but often preferred in academic writing.

> *It is difficult to <u>work,</u> <u>study,</u> **and** <u>take care</u> of small children at the same time.*

2. When words, phrases, or clauses are joined with the paired conjunctions *not only . . . but also, both . . . and, either . . . or,* or *neither . . . nor,* they must be parallel in form.

> **Not only** <u>farmers</u> **but also** <u>ranchers</u> are affected by agricultural policies. (nouns)

> **Both** <u>Jenny</u> **and** <u>Judy</u> play water polo. (nouns)

> *My son was* **neither** <u>anxious</u> **nor** <u>upset</u> *at the doctor's office.* (adjectives)

> *We will* **either** <u>see a movie</u> **or** <u>go out to dinner</u> *tonight.* (verb phrases)

3. When using the paired conjunction *not only . . . but also* to connect independent clauses, the word order is inverted if the sentence begins with *not only.* For verbs other than *be,* add an auxiliary verb after *not only.*

Regular word order:	<u>There is</u> **not only** *an apricot tree in the yard, but there is also a plum tree.*
Inverted word order:	**Not only** <u>is there</u> *an apricot tree in the yard, but there is also a plum tree.*
Regular word order:	<u>Debbie</u> **not only** <u>likes</u> *to swim, but she also likes to run.*
Inverted word order:	**Not only** <u>does Debbie like</u> *to swim, but she also likes to run.*

Self Check 2

Circle the sentence that uses parallel structure correctly.

1. (a) Vicki has improved her writing by learning grammar rules and editing carefully.

  (b) Vicki has improved her writing by learning grammar rules, and she edits carefully.

2. (a) Ms. Lee is searching for a new job and moves to a new house at the same time.

  (b) Ms. Lee is searching for a new job and moving to a new house at the same time.

3. (a) Anton is good at listening to problems, thinking about them, and always giving good advice.

  (b) Anton is good at listening to problems, thinking about them, and he always gives good advice.

4. (a) My roommate was neither nervous nor relax the night before the state board exam.

  (b) My roommate was neither nervous nor relaxed the night before the state board exam.

5. (a) I will either study painting or sculpture.

  (b) I will study either painting or sculpture.

EDITING PRACTICE

1. *Put a check (✓) next to the sentences that use coordination and parallel structure correctly. Correct the sentences that have errors.*

_____ **1.** Both fruits and vegetables are part of a healthy diet.

_____ **2.** Neither the play is entertaining nor funny.

_____ **3.** Expensive medical care keeps people from seeking medical services they

become sicker and medical costs increase.

_____ **4.** Not only did my grandmother teach me about generosity, but she also

taught me the meaning of happiness.

_____ **5.** Mr. Bustillo was very well prepared for the speech, so he didn't do a very

good job.

_____ **6.** Civil rights groups are not afraid to stand up for their beliefs and to

challenge those who disagree with them.

_____ **7.** Today's students cannot imagine working in a traditional nine-to-five

job and having only two weeks of vacation each year.

_____ **8.** Sissela loves science. So she is going to major in biology.

_____ **9.** Children learn a lot from storytelling important life lessons are taught

in an entertaining manner.

_____ **10.** The antique photograph illustrates the struggle, sacrifice, and hardship

that past generations experienced.

_____ **11.** When I received my diploma, my parents looked at me and smile.

_____ **12.** Either skiing in Canada or camping in New Zealand are my next

vacation.

2. *Read the following paragraph. Complete the paragraph with the correct coordinating conjunctions.*

Over the last decade _____ two, the development
                       1. or / and

of self-esteem has become a popular topic. In fact, it has become an

industry with thousands of books, seminars, _____
                                        2. or / and

dollars devoted to the building of self-esteem. Some of these sources

encourage people to visualize success, to repeat positive thoughts,

_____ to heal wounds from the past. Traditional thinking
     3. and / but

teaches that to be successful we cannot have too much self-doubt. This

may sound logical, _____ some people question this
                   4. but / and

approach to the development of self-esteem. They wonder which comes

first, self-esteem _____ success. They believe that
               5. and / or

people must first experience success before they can develop self-esteem,

_____ they will not feel good about themselves without
     6. yet / for

feeling successful. In other words, it's difficult to feel positive about ourselves

before we achieve success, _____ it is necessary to take risks
                 7. so / or

to increase self-worth. Furthermore, the anxiety we feel due to self-doubt can

be used in a positive way. If someone has a fear of flying, public speaking,

_____ taking a new job, he or she should do this activity
     8. yet / or

to get over the fear and to build self-esteem. It is also necessary to have goals,

_____ when feelings of doubt begin to get in the way, the
     9. so / but

direction _____ goal is still clear. Regardless of the approach
           10. for / or

one takes to gain self-esteem, most agree that it is necessary for a productive

and successful life.

3. *In the following essay, the underlined sentences have errors in coordination or parallel structure. Write your corrections above each underlined sentence.*

(1.) Human beings are social animals, but they still need a personal space to be alone, feel safe, and being in control. This space may be a neighborhood, a home, or a room. (2.) Or even half of a room! One of the reasons we feel secure in our space is because our personal possessions surround us. Studies show that people who have their belongings around them feel more attached to a particular spot than people who do not; this is especially true in dormitories where personal space is very limited. (3.) In a dormitory, both possessions show one's side of the room and one's personality or interests. (4.) Students decorate with personal items such as computers, they have pictures, and bring stuffed animals, so their new space will feel familiar to them. I have done this, too. (5.) I define my personal space, and help others know about me by putting up basketball posters of my favorite players. (6.) When people come into my room, they see my love of basketball, my admiration of some players. (7.) Not only I display my basketball posters, but I also have basketballs, basketball shoes, basketball jerseys, and basketball magazines on my half of the dorm room. (8.) I brought all these belongings from home, yet now I feel half of the dorm room is my own. This has helped me feel secure during my first months in a new environment. (9.) We can easily see the many ways that people personalize their home and office spaces but this human need is the most obvious in the small space of a dormitory room. (10.) We all like to believe we are unique, for we all have the same need to have a personal space of our own.

4. *The following paragraphs have ten errors in the formal use of coordination and parallel structure. Find and correct the errors.*

The definition of the term power is the control or influence that individuals or groups hold over others. Some examples of power include the authority of parents over children, the physical force of one person over another, and when large countries have influence over small countries. Love can even be a form of power. Some people give or withholding their love so that they get what they want from another person. All these kinds of power can be used in a negative way, it is possible to use them wisely. This is especially true with the power of love.

My parents used their love as a form of power over me when I was a senior in high school. I always knew my parents had authority over me, so I had never realized this power was a result of their love. They used their love powerfully when it was time for me to select a college. I had been working hard for four years to be accepted at a good college, yet I was thrilled when my acceptance letter arrived. When my parents realized that I would be studying hundreds of miles from home, they used their power to encourage me to select another university closer to our city. Although I had worked, dream, and planning to attend my first-choice university, I almost gave up my dream for my parents. Their love was a strong influence over me. But I knew what I wanted. Not only I stood up against their power, but I also changed their minds about my decision. Both my parents and I now know that I made

the right decision by leaving home, but it was difficult for my parents to see

their influence decrease in my life. It was an educational experience for me to

observe the power of love and learning how to use it well.

WRITING TOPICS

Study the student paragraph that uses coordination and parallel structure. Circle three different coordinating or correlative conjunctions and underline two uses of parallel structure in the paragraph.

Most academic paragraphs, whether they are part of an essay or stand alone, include a clear topic sentence, a body, and a concluding sentence. Notice that this paragraph has these three important parts of an academic paragraph. Use this paragraph as a model when you write about one of the topics below.

Apple Inc. produces the most effective advertisements in the media today. The primary reason for Apple's success is the simplicity and creativity of its advertisements. The ads for Apple products contain very few images and words, yet they convey a very strong message. On both television and billboard advertisements, there is usually one very simple image of a person using an Apple product. However, this one image shows how to use the product, what the product can do, and why it will make the user's life better. One simple image provides so much information about a product and its user. Not only does Apple use simplicity to sell its products, but it also demonstrates the creativity of the people who use Apple technology. The people in the ads—their actions, clothing, and location—clearly show their creativity. Apple convinces us that these are the type of people that we all want to be. Apple's advertising campaign is effective, so millions of people around the world buy their products and have made this company one of the most influential in the world.

Choose one of the topics below and write at least one paragraph. Be sure to use parallel structure and several different coordinating conjunctions. After you complete your first draft, concentrate on editing your work. Keep in mind the editing practice from this chapter.

1. Many people prefer to read fiction while others read only nonfiction. Which do you prefer to read? Explain why you like one type of writing over the other and give examples of stories, novels, or articles that you have enjoyed.

2. Carefully describe an advertisement that you have recently seen or heard. The advertisement could be from television, radio, magazines, billboards, or any other source. Explain why this advertisement caught your eye and why you think it is particularly effective or ineffective.

Go to page 152 for more practice with coordination and parallel structure.

Adjective Clauses

GRAMMAR FOCUS

Adjective clauses, also called relative clauses, are like adjectives because they identify or give information about nouns or pronouns. You can use adjective clauses to combine sentences and to make your writing more descriptive and interesting. Compare these two examples:

(A) *We love the old house. It has a huge pear tree.*

(B) *We love the old house* **that has a huge pear tree**.

Both examples have the same meaning, but example B uses an adjective clause and expresses the same information with fewer words and in a more complex and interesting way than example A.

Pretest

Check your understanding of adjective clauses. Put a check (✓) next to the sentences that are correct.

____ 1. The company that I want to work for provides good benefits.

____ 2. The book is overdue that I borrowed from the library.

____ 3. Countries whose gun laws are strict have few gun deaths.

____ 4. Alan's father, which has a Ph.D. in chemical engineering, has high expectations for his son.

____ 5. The movie's hero, who is in the first half of the film, unexpectedly disappears in the second half.

____ 6. My friends recommended the restaurant that is on the corner of Irvine Avenue and Seventeenth Street.

____ 7. Countries, that have earthquakes, need strict building codes.

____ 8. Dr. Kaufman who teaches physiology will retire soon.

____ 9. The concert tickets that Carol and I bought them are in my purse.

____ 10. The winter Jan worked at the ski resort was the best of her life.

The following paragraph contains adjective clauses. Two adjective clauses are underlined. Find at least two more examples of adjective clauses in the paragraph and underline them.

Most countries have one or two official languages, but there may be many citizens <u>whose first language is not one of these official languages</u>. This is certainly true in India, where two official languages and hundreds of regional languages exist. Hindi, <u>which many Indians speak</u>, is the principal language of the country, while English, which was the official language of British India, is the secondary language. In addition, each state within the country has its own official language. Language commissions that monitor disputes and create language policies have been established to reduce problems that develop because of so many different languages. The different scripts that accompany different languages are another challenge that India faces. Although diverse languages can cause problems within a country such as India, they are also one reason that India is such an interesting country to study and visit.

FORMING ADJECTIVE CLAUSES

1. An adjective clause is a dependent clause, which means it cannot stand alone. It must be connected to an independent, or main, clause. A sentence that contains a dependent clause and an independent clause is called a complex sentence. An adjective clause is introduced by a relative pronoun such as *that, who, whom, which,* or *whose.* The noun or pronoun that the relative pronoun refers to is called the antecedent.

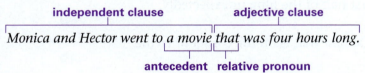

       independent clause   **adjective clause**

Monica and Hector went to a movie that was four hours long.

        antecedent   relative pronoun

2. In most cases, the adjective clause directly follows the noun it is identifying or describing (the antecedent).

The surprise birthday <u>party</u> **that Grant and Bob gave for Stella** *was a lot of fun.*

                      not

The surprise birthday party was a lot of fun that Grant and Bob gave for Stella.

The <u>man</u> **who(m) we spoke to** *gave us good advice.*

              not

The man gave us good advice who(m) we spoke to.

3. Do not repeat the noun or pronoun (the antecedent) within the adjective clause.

Joanna's father is <u>the kind of person</u> **who never gets mad**.

not

Joanna's father is the kind of person who he never gets mad.

This is <u>the program</u> **that Samuel and I wrote for our computer science class**.

not

This is the program that Samuel and I wrote it for our computer science class.

4. When a relative pronoun is the subject of the adjective clause, use a subject pronoun.

- *who* or *that* for people

  Susanna baby-sits for her neighbor. Her neighbor has five children. ⟶ Susanna baby-sits for her neighbor **who has five children**.

  The girls live next door. The girls are really nice. ⟶ The girls **that live next door** are really nice.

- *which* or *that* for things

  John wrote a research paper. The research paper analyzes the causes of depression. ⟶ John wrote a research paper **that analyzes the causes of depression**.

  In political science, we read The Prince. The Prince *was written in the early 1500s*. ⟶ In political science, we read The Prince, **which was written in the early 1500s**.

5. When a relative pronoun is the object of the adjective clause, use an object pronoun.

- *whom, who,* or *that* for people

  Harry Truman governed during the late 1940s. My grandmother knew Harry Truman. ⟶ Harry Truman, **who(m) my grandmother knew**, *governed during the late 1940s.*

- *which* or *that* for things

  Abby bought a computer yesterday. The computer will be delivered to the store tomorrow. ⟶ The computer **that Abby bought yesterday** *will be delivered to the store tomorrow.*

- A relative pronoun can also be the object of a preposition.

  The car **that Rose left her purse in** *was stolen.*

  The car **in which Rose left her purse** *was stolen.* (formal, academic English)

NOTE: When the relative pronoun is the object of the verb or object of a preposition, it can be omitted.

The computer **that** Abby bought yesterday will be delivered tomorrow. (That is the object of the verb bought.) ⟶ The computer Abby bought yesterday will be delivered tomorrow.

The car **that** Rose left her purse in was stolen. (That is the object of the preposition in.) ⟶ The car Rose left her purse in was stolen.

6. When a relative pronoun replaces a possessive word, use whose + noun.

<u>My sister's son</u> just went away to college. My sister feels lonely. ⟶ My sister, **whose son** just went away to college, feels lonely.

The <u>company's headquarters</u> are in Boston. The company has offices in North America, Europe, and Asia. ⟶ The company, **whose headquarters** are in Boston, has offices in North America, Europe, and Asia.

WRITING TIP

In spoken English, *whose* and *who's* sound similar. In writing, be sure to use the contraction *who's* for *who is* and *who has* and the relative pronoun *whose* to show possession.

Who's going to the graduation ceremony?

Russell found the child **who's** been missing for a week.

I want to work for a company **whose** profits are increasing.

---

7. Sentences with adjective clauses must follow all subject-verb agreement rules.

- The subject and verb of the independent clause must agree even if they are separated by an adjective clause.

  The chemistry **classes** <u>that I took last semester</u> **were** very interesting.

  > not

  The chemistry classes that I took last semester was very interesting.

- The verb following the relative pronoun always has the same number (singular or plural) as the antecedent.

  Our neighbors have a <u>dog</u> **that barks** all day long. (singular)

  The <u>boys</u> in my dorm **who play** water polo travel a lot with the team. (plural)

- The subject and verb within the relative clause must agree.

  The textbooks that she is buying cost $250.
           S   V

  > not

  The textbooks that she are buying cost $250.

WRITING TIP

When you write, mark the subjects and verbs in sentences that use adjective clauses. Put the letter *S* below subjects and the letter *V* below verbs, and check that each pair agrees.

---

8. Restrictive adjective clauses (also called identifying or defining clauses) do not require commas. A restrictive adjective clause supplies necessary information to identify the noun that it modifies. Restrictive adjective clauses are used more frequently than nonrestrictive adjective clauses.

   A __person__ **who sells stocks and bonds** *is called a stockbroker.*

   (The information in the adjective clause is necessary in order to know which person is being described.)

   Do you know the __man__ **who is at the table** *in the corner?*

   (The information in the adjective clause is necessary in order to know which man is being referred to.)

9. Nonrestrictive adjective clauses (also called nonidentifying or nondefining clauses) require commas. A nonrestrictive clause supplies additional information that is not necessary to identify the noun it modifies.

   We just read One Hundred Years of Solitude**, which is by Gabriel Garcia Marquez**.

   (The additional information in the adjective clause is not necessary to identify the book.)

   My oldest sister, **who lives in Chicago,** *loves the cold weather there.*

   (The additional information in the adjective clause is not necessary to identify which sister.)

NOTE: Do not use the relative pronoun *that* in a nonrestrictive adjective clause.

   Old Faithful, **which** *is located in Yellowstone National Park, regularly shoots water and steam into the air.*

   not

   Old Faithful, that is located in Yellowstone National Park, regularly shoots water and steam into the air.

10. With proper nouns, always use nonrestrictive adjective clauses.

   Ten Downing Street, **where the prime minister of England lives,** *is a plain-looking house.*

11. Commas around an adjective clause can change the meaning of a sentence. Compare the meanings of the following sentences:

   The students, **who wanted to study French,** *had to wait in line to register.*

   (The use of commas means that all of the students wanted to study French, and all of them had to wait in line.)

   The students **who wanted to study French** *had to wait in line to register. The students* **who wanted to study German** *didn't have to wait in line.*

   (The lack of commas means that only some of the students wanted to study French. The adjective clause identifies which students had to wait in line.)

NOTE: Adjective clauses can be used to describe indefinite pronouns such as *someone, anyone, everything,* and *other.* However, adjective clauses cannot be used to describe subject and object pronouns such as *he, she, him,* or *her.*

   Someone **who wanted to speak with you** *called but didn't leave a message.*

   I don't know anyone **who has a truck**.

USING ADJECTIVE CLAUSES

1. Use adjective clauses to combine ideas. This creates sentences that are less repetitive.

> *My best friend is a medical student. She hopes to specialize in pediatrics.*

> *My best friend,* **who is a medical student***, hopes to specialize in pediatrics.*

2. Use adjective clauses to make general sentences more specific or descriptive.

General	*They just finished a research project.*
Descriptive	*They just finished a research project* **that discusses the effectiveness of grammar instruction in reading classes***.*

3. The relative adverbs *where* and *when* can be used to introduce adjective clauses of place and time.

> *We went to Yellowstone,* **where** *we saw Old Faithful.*

> *The week* **when** *she was in the hospital was hard on her parents.*

WRITING TIP

In academic and business writing, the language tends to be more formal than in other kinds of writing. If you are writing for a college or university class, try to use the more formal forms of English. Notice the different levels of formality in these adjective clauses.

Least formal	The person I feel closest **to** is my sister.	This is the book I told you **about**.
	The person that I feel closest **to** is my sister.	This is the book that I told you **about**.
	The person who(m) I feel closest **to** is my sister.	This is the book which I told you **about**.
Most formal	The person **to** whom I feel closest is my sister.	This is the book **about** which I told you.

Self Check

Circle the sentence that uses adjective clauses correctly.

1. (a) Ethan's uncle which teaches economics is a fair grader.

(b) Ethan's uncle who teaches economics is a fair grader. ✓

2. (a) Samuel Clemens who wrote *Tom Sawyer* used the pen name Mark Twain.

(b) Samuel Clemens, who wrote *Tom Sawyer*, used the pen name Mark Twain. ✓

3. (a) The classes Sam is taking begin next week. ✓

(b) The classes Sam is taking begins next week.

4. (a) The interview that I had yesterday with the director went well. ✓

(b) The interview with the director went well that I had yesterday.

5. (a) They went to a wedding ceremony that it was on the beach at sunset.

(b) They went to a wedding ceremony that was on the beach at sunset. ✓

EDITING PRACTICE

1. *Put a check (✓) next to the sentences that use adjective clauses correctly. Correct the sentences that have errors.*

_____ 1. Thoa's father, which used to play college football, is coaching a high school team.

_____ 2. The blending of cultures that we see in the United States today has both advantages and disadvantages.

_____ 3. The bulbs should bloom in the spring that we planted last winter.

_____ 4. The ABC Software Company whose president just resigned is in financial trouble.

_____ 5. St. John, which is a Caribbean island, is a tropical paradise.

_____ 6. The 1992 demonstration that we are going to study it in sociology was very destructive.

_____ 7. Extremely competitive people who always have to win has difficulty in their relationships.

_____ 8. The woman whom the story is about lives in a small New England town.

_____ 9. Galileo Galilei, whom never left Italy, is nonetheless known around the world.

_____ 10. The Tasman Sea, where the poisonous box jellyfish lives, is the home of several deadly sea creatures.

_____ 11. The Puerto Rican culture which Esmeralda Santiago writes about in *When I Was Puerto Rican* has not changed significantly in the past few decades.

_____ 12. Professor Williams, whose class is on Wednesday nights, is an excellent writing teacher.

2. Read the following paragraph. Complete the paragraph with the correct relative pronoun, relative adverb, or neither (Ø).

D.H. Lawrence celebrates old age in his poem *Beautiful Old Age*. Although old age is a stage of life _____ is not

1. when / that

always valued, Lawrence writes about some of its positive points. He says that a person

_____ has led a truthful life

2. who / which

will live happily into old age. Old age should

be a time _____ people feel

3. when / where

peace from having lived a full life. Wrinkled

skin, _____ is unavoidable, is a sign of wisdom and not of

4. that / which

deterioration. If people believe Lawrence's words, then maturity ought to be

a stage _____ we look forward to, and the elderly person

5. who / that

_____ we fear becoming ought to be looked at as someone

6. Ø / which

_____ we hope to be. Two people _____

7. Ø / where   **8. whom / who**

fit this description of beautiful old age are my great-grandmother and my

great-aunt. Both women have lived honest lives _____

9. when / that

have been filled with hard work and family. They are being rewarded for

their work as their children, grandchildren, and great-grandchildren honor

them daily. This is the old age that I hope to have one day—the old age that

D.H. Lawrence describes and the old age _____ my great-

10. when / that

grandmother and great-aunt are living.

3. In the following paragraph, five of the underlined adjective clauses are not correct. Find the errors and write the corrections above each clause.

There are many examples of the cultural influences <u>that powerful countries have on less powerful countries</u>. The British influence in Antigua,
1

the French influence in Vietnam, and the American influence in Puerto Rico are all examples of less dominant cultures following the styles and traditions of more dominant cultures. According to Jamacia Kincaid, who is an Antiguan writer, the native gardens <u>that grow in Antigua</u> are wild and natural. However,
2

the British influence, <u>that many wealthy Antiguans admire</u>, is obvious in the
3

island's gardens. Christmas trees <u>which originated in Germany</u> have also
4

found their way to Antigua due to the British influence. In Vietnam, the

French influence, <u>which was more apparent years ago</u>, is still obvious today.
5

Vietnamese food and architecture, which are considered traditional, have a

French touch. The French language, <u>which was the language of the educated</u>
6

<u>and influential</u>, still holds a position of importance in Vietnam. In Puerto

Rico, Americans have influenced the language. Spanish, <u>that is the primary</u>
7

<u>language in Puerto Rico</u>, has been replaced by English in some schools and

institutions. In addition to the English language, American food and music

are now part of the Puerto Rican way of life. Many can still remember several

decades ago <u>when Americans came to their small towns to "educate" them</u>
8

<u>about diet and hygiene</u>. Many Puerto Ricans <u>whom accepted this influence at</u>
9

<u>the time</u> were unhappy about it later. In this day and age, it is hard to stop or

even to ignore worldwide influences. However, outside cultural influence is a

phenomenon <u>who's importance should be questioned</u>.
10

4. *The following paragraph has ten errors in the use of adjective clauses. Find and correct the errors.*

The object that I am looking at is a three-dimensional rectangle,

although sometimes this object can be in the shape of a cube or a sphere. Five

sides are made of glass, that is clear, and there is either a removable top or

no top at all. One usually finds this object in a room when people are likely

to meet, such as the living room, family room, or kitchen. This object is not

mobile. It often has a small motor that keep the environment clean. However,

the object still has to be cleaned every few weeks. Plants may also be found

inside of it that help keep this object clean. Next to the plants, there are

sometimes figurines that they are set in brightly colored rocks. Both adults

and children like this object. Some people who they have stressful lives find

this object peaceful to look at. People whom have these objects usually love

animals. Animals use this object for a home that live in fresh and salt water.

The animals, that live in this object, make good pets for a person who he is

allergic to cats and dogs. Do you know what this object is?

WRITING TOPICS

Study the student paragraph that uses adjective clauses. Circle the five adjective clauses in this paragraph.

Most academic paragraphs, whether they are part of an essay or stand alone, include a clear topic sentence, a body, and a concluding sentence. Notice that this paragraph has these three important parts of an academic paragraph. Use this paragraph as a model when you write about one of the topics below.

A jock is a person who loves to play sports. A jock can also be called a sportsperson or an athlete. There are many positive attributes of a jock. An athlete who works hard at his sport may be considered a jock. It takes a lot of focus and determination, which are positive traits, to be a good sportsperson. Jocks also have to take the advice of their coaches and be good listeners. These are characteristics that make good employees, friends, and spouses in the future. However, some negative stereotypes are also associated with jocks. Sometimes jocks are not considered intelligent. Because they focus on their sport rather than their education, some people think they are dumb. They may also use their muscles rather than their heads to solve problems. This kind of behavior makes jocks look emotional and irrational at times. Even though the term "jock" is just another word for "athlete," it carries many positive and negative impressions that a simple word may not have.

Choose one of the topics below and write at least one paragraph. Be sure to use adjective clauses. After you complete your first draft, concentrate on editing your work. Keep in mind the editing practice from this chapter.

1. Write a description or definition of a slang term such as *nerd, wimp, chicken,* or *know-it-all*. These terms show unique characteristics of the people that they describe. Choose one of these terms or one of your own and explain the meaning of this word by using clear examples.

2. How is the education that you are receiving now different from the education you received as a child or in another country? Discuss differences such as those you find in social life, academic pressure, testing, grading, and extracurricular activities.

Go to page 154 for more practice with adjective clauses.

Adverb Clauses

GRAMMAR FOCUS

Adverb clauses allow you to describe relationships such as those showing comparison and contrast, time, and cause and effect. They also help you combine short sentences into longer, complex sentences that show the relationship between the two. Compare examples (A) and (B). With the adverb clause, sentence (B) reads more smoothly and emphasizes the contrast expressed in the two original sentences.

(A) I finished the novel that you recommended. I didn't like it very much.

(B) I finished the novel that you recommended, **even though I didn't like it very much**.

Pretest

Check your understanding of adverb clauses. Put a check (✓) next to the sentences that are correct.

_____ **1.** Since I found a parking space close to my classroom, I didn't make it to class on time.

_____ **2.** Even though it is difficult and expensive to travel to the Arctic Circle it is worth the effort.

_____ **3.** Although Suri studied for the quiz, but she received a low grade.

_____ **4.** That actress is so well known that being in public places is difficult for her.

_____ **5.** While we were studying at Kylie's house last night.

_____ **6.** Mr. and Mrs. Skinner will live wherever they can easily visit their grandchildren.

_____ **7.** We have enjoyed watching television since we got a new TV.

_____ **8.** Ronaldo doesn't feel comfortable in the ocean due to he has only swum in swimming pools.

_____ **9.** After they were married, they moved to a new apartment.

_____ **10.** The Flynns traveled to Ireland last summer so that they could visit family there.

The following paragraph contains adverb clauses. Two complex sentences with adverb clauses are underlined. Find two more examples of adverb clauses in the paragraph and underline them.

Competition for a limited amount of water may be one of the biggest problems that future generations face. <u>Although the Earth is 97 percent water, only 3 percent is usable freshwater.</u> Limited water resources combined with the problem of water pollution have been called a *water crisis* by some organizations and governments. <u>As developing countries with large populations gain additional access to freshwater, more shortages will begin to occur.</u> In developed and developing countries, good governance is the key to lessening a water crisis in the future. A variety of solutions exist, but many are so expensive that they are difficult for developing countries to afford. Because a future water crisis will be a global problem, the solution lies in cooperation among all nations.

FORMING COMPLEX SENTENCES WITH ADVERB CLAUSES

1. An adverb clause is a dependent clause that begins with a subordinating conjunction such as *because, after,* or *although.* An adverb clause must be connected to an independent, or main, clause. Remember that a sentence that contains a dependent clause and an independent clause is called a complex sentence. See below the complex sentences that contain adverb clauses and the rules for forming them that follow.

independent clause	adverb clause

I don't understand the concept because it is very complicated.

subordinating conjunction

adverb clause	independent clause

After it rained for a week, there was a lot of pollution in the bay.

subordinating conjunction

2. An adverb clause cannot stand alone. It must be attached to an independent clause or a fragment results.

Complete sentence:	*We lived in the city* **before we moved to the mountains.**
Fragment:	*Before we moved to the mountains.*
Complete sentence:	**Although the weather forecast isn't good,** *I think we should go to the beach.*
Fragment:	*Although the weather forecast isn't good.*

3. Use a comma after an adverb clause that begins a sentence.

Although Armando is working in the business world, *he hopes to move into education soon.*

Do not use a comma when the independent clause comes before the adverb clause.

My daughter will never have a large salary **because she wants to be a forest ranger**.

NOTE: If the independent clause is followed by an adverb that shows contrast or concession (*although, though, even though, while,* or *whereas*), a comma may separate the clauses.

Antonio is an excellent writing student, **whereas** *Emi is a very poor writing student.*

4. Subordinating conjunctions cannot be combined with other conjunctions within the same sentence.

Even though *we didn't speak the language, we were able to communicate well.*

not

Even though we didn't speak the language, but we were able to communicate well.

5. Do not use a prepositional phrase instead of a subordinating conjunction. A prepositional phrase cannot be used to connect two clauses.

Because the wind was blowing so hard, the tree in our front yard fell over.

subordinating conjunction

not

Because of the wind was blowing so hard, the tree in our front yard fell over.

6. Place the conjunction in the correct clause. The subordinating conjunction belongs in the clause that shows its relationship with the independent clause.

When *Jason's clothes get too tight, he goes on a diet.*

not

Jason's clothes get too tight when he goes on a diet.

USING ADVERB CLAUSES

1. Use adverb clauses to emphasize the relationship between ideas and to connect short sentences. Notice that a subordinating conjunction makes one idea less important than the other.   *not equal.*

He washed his car for the first time in two months. (independent clause)

He has a date tonight. (independent clause)

He washed his car for the first time in two months. (independent clause, more important)

because he has a date tonight. (adverb clause, less important)

2. Subordinating conjunctions can be categorized according to their meaning.

TIME		
after	before	when
as	since	whenever
as soon as	until	while

We decided to serve dinner **after** our guests had arrived.

As soon as the plums are ripe, I am going to make jam.

NOTE: *Until* means that something happens up to a specific point in time and then stops.

They were living in Arizona **until** they moved to Wyoming.

Until the tornado passes, we will be down in the basement.

REASON/CAUSE	
as	due to the fact that
because	since

Since Katya loves dogs, we bought her a puppy for her birthday.

The old oak tree died **due to the fact that** it had root disease.

CONCESSION		
although	even though	though
despite the fact that	in spite of the fact that	

We loved the movie **even though** all the reviews were bad.

Although the temperature is below freezing, my children love to play outside.

CONTRAST	
whereas	while

We took the train and arrived in one hour, **whereas** Pete drove and arrived in thirty minutes.

While Tom is a good math student and a poor English student, Pam does well in English and poorly in math.

NOTE: Subordinating conjunctions of contrast are used for actions or situations that are in direct opposition or contrast, whereas subordinating conjunctions of concession are used for actions or situations that show surprising or unexpected results.

RESULT	
so . . . that	such . . . that

I was **so** busy **that** I forgot to wish her a happy birthday. (adjective)

Marta drives **so** quickly **that** her friends don't like to drive with her. (adverb)

We had **such** a busy day **that** we were late for dinner. (noun phrase)

PURPOSE	
in order that	so that

Fatima wants to move closer to school **so that** she doesn't spend so much time commuting.

In order that we don't pay a fine, we must get our taxes in on time.

PLACE	
where	wherever

I will move **wherever** I get a job.

This city has a swimming pool **where** he can swim laps.

3. The conjunction must create a logical relationship between the ideas in the sentence.

   Incorrect or illogical: Brandon sucked his thumb **because** he was three years old.

(Brandon's age is not the reason that he sucked his thumb. Many three-year-olds do not suck their thumbs.)

   Correct or logical: Brandon sucked his thumb **because** he was tired.

   Correct or logical: Brandon sucked his thumb **until** he was three years old.

   Incorrect or illogical: Most students have to study **while** they can pass their classes.

(Passing a class is usually the result of studying. *While* shows contrast or time, neither of which is a logical choice in this sentence.)

   Correct or logical: Most students have to study **so that** they can pass their classes.

   Correct or logical: Most students have to study **while** they are in school.

4. Some conjunctions (e.g., *as, since, while*) have more than one meaning.

as	**As** *Paul and Elina were leaving the house, the phone rang.* (time)
	My older cousin received many scholarships **as** *he was the best student in his school.* (reason/cause)
since	*It has not rained* **since** *the last time they went camping.* (time)
	Since *Cyrus and Jasmin are neighbors, they should get to know each other better.* (reason/cause)
while	**While** *the Trans were on vacation, their house was robbed.* (time)
	My little sister loves vegetables, **while** *most children dislike them.* (contrast)

WRITING TIP

Good writers end sentences with the clause that most logically leads to the idea in the next sentence. Think about the flow or coherence of your ideas as you edit, especially with complex sentences.

Self Check

Circle the sentence that uses adverb clauses correctly.

1. (a) Amy had so a good time at the party that she didn't want to leave.

   (b) Amy had such a good time at the party that she didn't want to leave.

2. (a) Ana Marie rides the bus to school so that she will have to worry about parking her car.

   (b) Ana Marie rides the bus to school so that she will not have to worry about parking her car.

3. (a) Even though the pool was warm, we decided not to go swimming.

   (b) Even though the pool was warm, but we decided not to go swimming.

4. (a) Mitchell has to graduate soon because of he is running out of money for tuition.

   (b) Mitchell has to graduate soon because he is running out of money for tuition.

5. (a) After my sister spent hours writing her essay, she received an A on it.

   (b) After my sister spent hours writing her essay she received an A on it.

EDITING PRACTICE

1. *Put a check (✓) next to the sentences that use adverb clauses correctly. Correct the sentences that have errors.*

_____ **1.** Because the class didn't agree with the teacher's grading system, we had to follow it.

_____ **2.** Though Jane doesn't like the sweater her grandmother gave her she wears it often.

_____ **3.** It's important to place plants where they can get sufficient sun and water.

_____ **4.** Since I live across the street from school and eat all my meals at home.

_____ **5.** Dr. Dubus prefers to travel by train, while most people prefer to fly nowadays.

_____ **6.** My dad turned on the air conditioner so that the temperature would be comfortable.

_____ **7.** We read that book last semester though it was a requirement of the course.

_____ **8.** We have no food in the house because we are hungry.

_____ **9.** Although the price of electricity is increasing, but we continue to consume more of it.

_____ **10.** The tour group traveled to so a high altitude that many people became sick.

_____ **11.** Due to the fact that Gilbert's unhealthy diet, he gained ten pounds last semester.

_____ **12.** I will study English until I pass the TOEFL.

2. *Read the following paragraph. Complete the paragraph with the correct subordinating conjunction.*

Last summer I bought an old Vespa motor scooter and restored it

to its original condition. I almost did not begin this project because I

was _____ shocked at the price of thirty-year-old
           1. so / such

scooters that I almost didn't buy mine. _____ I
                               2. While / Before

found my scooter, I had looked at dozens of others. Although mine needed

a lot of work, _____ I chose my particular Vespa
            3. even though / Ø

_____ this model is considered the peak of Vespa
    4. since / even though

design. _____ I was restoring my Vespa over the
      5. While / Although

summer, I went to scooter shows and shops where I met a lot of nice people

who were also scooter enthusiasts. _____ I met these
                       6. Though / Since

people, I have joined the Vespa Club, gone on several rallies, and made many

new friends. My scooter has really influenced my life. I don't think I will

ever sell my scooter _____ I could lose touch with the
             7. because / though

interesting people I have met. Other people may soon share my enthusiasm

for scooters _____ the Vespa company is selling
    8. due to the fact that / due to

Vespas worldwide again. _____ you see Vespas for sale,
            9. Until / Wherever

you should take one for a test drive _____ you can
              10. Ø / so that

experience the fun of riding a scooter.

3. *In the following paragraphs, ten words or phrases are underlined. In six places, either the underlined item or the following adverb clause is wrong. Correct each error.*

The importance of language is obvious but also mysterious. On the surface, language allows people to communicate, but it also holds people's culture, values, and ideals together. <u>When</u> a group of people loses or begins
1
to lose its language, more than just a tool of communication is lost. One example of this is <u>whenever</u> Korea was declared a protectorate and annexed as
2
a Japanese colony in 1905 after the Russo-Japanese War. Koreans were forbidden to use the Korean language in schools and public areas. Even though the Korean language survived, <u>but</u> Koreans were set apart from one
3
another <u>because of</u> they could no longer use their own language. <u>Wherever</u>
4   **5**
colonization has taken place throughout the world, we can observe similar situations.

Languages are not always lost as a result of colonization or physical domination. <u>Due to</u> English is spreading all over the world, many languages
6
are fighting to survive. People who live in countries with small populations must speak English <u>so that</u> they can communicate with the outside world.
7
The people of Wales are a perfect example of this. Welsh was spoken by <u>so</u> a
8
small number of people <u>that</u> it was on the verge of extinction. <u>As soon as</u> the
9
Welsh realized that they might lose their language, they fought to save it.
<u>Because</u> language holds so much cultural significance. All languages, no
10
matter how narrowly spoken, must be kept alive.

4. *The following paragraph has ten errors in the use of adverb clauses, including punctuation. Find and correct the errors.*

In the short story "The Catbird Seat," James Thurber, the author, uses humor to write about some common problems that exist between men and women. In this story, we see Mr. Martin's anger toward his new female colleague, Mrs. Barrows. Mr. Martin is a boring man who is used to a strict routine so that Mrs. Barrows's is just the opposite. Wherever Mrs. Barrows goes in the office, she introduces a lot of changes. Because of Mr. Martin feels Mrs. Barrows' main goal is to disrupt his ordinary life, a battle between the two follows. Since Mrs. Barrows doesn't realize it, she has also angered her other coworkers. Mr. Martin is so upset that he decides his only option is to murder Mrs. Barrows. Before Mr. Martin decides to commit murder he has never broken his daily routine of work, dinner, and two glasses of milk before bed. Even though Mr. Martin's decision goes against his nature, but he feels there is no other solution. Until someone thinks up a better way to get rid of Mrs. Barrows. Mr. Martin is going to continue planning her murder. Finally, he comes up with a better idea than murder since this new plan is still not completely ethical. Mr. Martin feels that Mrs. Barrows is so a horrible person that his actions are justified. Despite the fact that Mrs. Barrows is a difficult person, she has good intentions. Mr. Martin fails to see this side of her personality due to he is sure she will destroy his daily routine. Although this is a humorous story. It is too bad that strong women like Mrs. Barrows are often portrayed in a negative light.

WRITING TOPICS

Study the student paragraph that uses adverb clauses. Circle the four adverb clauses that you find in this paragraph.

Most academic paragraphs, whether they are part of an essay or stand alone, include a clear topic sentence, a body, and a concluding sentence. Notice that this paragraph has these three important parts of an academic paragraph. Use this paragraph as a model when you write about one of the topics below.

Like diet and exercise, sleep is an important factor that affects our mental and physical health. In order that people perform their best, sleep is a necessity, not a luxury. Most of us have felt the physical effects of too little sleep. The first obvious physical signs might be muscle aches, headaches, dizziness, and memory loss. In the long term, sleep deprivation might lead to serious physical illnesses such as diabetes, high blood pressure, and obesity. While sleep deprivation negatively affects people's physical health, its effects may be more severe on mental health. When people do not have enough sleep for long periods of time, some mental illnesses are more likely to occur. People require sleep so that their brains can logically respond to events and appropriately regulate their moods. Sufficient sleep helps us control our levels of stress and improve our learning abilities. Basic lifestyle choices and daily habits like getting enough sleep play a big role in both our mental and physical health.

Choose one of the topics below and write at least one paragraph. Be sure to use adverb clauses. After you complete your first draft, concentrate on editing your work. Keep in mind the editing practice from this chapter.

1. Although the roles of men and women in society are changing, each gender is still governed by traditional rules and expectations. Compare the traditional male and female roles in two countries. Contrast these roles with the more modern rules and expectations that men and women follow today.

2. Explain how our mental health and/or physical health are affected by our daily habits and lifestyle choices. Describe how people feel and look when they have healthy habits versus unhealthy habits.

Go to page 156 for more practice with adverb clauses.

Conditionals

GRAMMAR FOCUS

Conditional sentences allow you to describe cause-and-effect relationships, to show possibility in the future, and to rethink the past. There are four basic patterns of conditional sentences. Each pattern has a different combination of verbs that must be formed correctly in order to convey the meaning you want.

For example, in the conditional sentence "If we spoke Chinese, we would consider moving to Beijing," the simple past is used in the *if* clause and the modal *would* is used in the independent clause. This conditional sentence conveys the meaning that we do not speak Chinese, so we are not likely to move to Beijing.

Pretest

Check your understanding of conditional sentences. Put a check (✓) next to the sentences that are correct.

____ **1.** If Joaquin buys a new car this year, he gets a hybrid.

____ **2.** The skiing is always good if the mountains get a lot of snow.

____ **3.** Daniel has always been a bad driver, and his driving skills show no sign of improving. If he begins to drive better, we will feel safer in his car.

____ **4.** Studies show that if people exercised daily, they will feel better.

____ **5.** If the two variables are equal and show the expected result.

____ **6.** I would volunteer at a homeless shelter if I have more time.

____ **7.** If we had invested in the stock market earlier, we would be better off today.

____ **8.** Eddy and Melinda will definitely be selected for the leading roles unless they forget their lines.

____ **9.** If I were you, I will move to Hawaii and live near the beach.

____ **10.** The mayor would have had our support if he had changed his policies on the environment.

The following information from a class syllabus contains conditional sentences. Underline the conditional clause and circle the result clause in each sentence. The first one has been done for you.

Students must follow several important rules to pass this class.

1. <u>If students turn in assignments late,</u> (they will lose 50 percent from the grade.)

2. If students are absent more than three times, the instructor may drop them from the class.

3. Students may not make up tests unless they are sick on the day of the test.

4. Students will get an A in the class if they receive 90 percent or higher on all coursework.

5. When students write an essay or short paragraph, it must be typed.

6. If students completed all extra credit assignments, they would receive an extra 10 percent on their grade.

FORMING CONDITIONALS

1. A conditional sentence has an *if* clause (adverb clause) and a result clause (independent clause). The *if* clause shows the necessary condition for the particular result.

    adverb clause   **independent clause**

    If *Bruno trains hard, he can finish the race.*

    independent clause   **adverb clause**

    My father will start a fire in the fireplace if it rains.

2. The *if* clause, like any other adverb clause used alone, is a fragment. It must be attached to an independent clause.

    Complete sentence: **If we studied more,** *we would get better grades.*

    Fragment: *If we studied more.*

    Complete sentence: *Coco and I don't want to go sailing* **if there is no wind.**

    Fragment: *If there is no wind.*

3. The *if* clause can come before or after the independent clause; however, the punctuation is different. When a sentence begins with an *if* clause, the clause is followed by a comma. When the *if* clause comes second, no comma is required.

    Comma: **If she decides to be a teacher,** *she will have a good life.*

    No comma: *She will have a good life* **if she decides to be a teacher.**

    Comma: **If you had done your homework,** *you could go out with us now.*

    No comma: *You could go out with us now* **if you had done your homework.**

4. In addition to *if*, conjunctions such as *unless* and *even if* are used in conditional sentences.

> **Unless** *it rains, the dance will be held outside.*

> *We are going on our trip* **even if** *it snows.*

USING CONDITIONALS

1. Use conditional sentences to show cause-and-effect relationships. The *if* clause shows a condition or cause, and the independent clause shows the result or effect.

> condition   result
>
> *If Heidi doesn't get good grades, she won't get a car for her eighteenth birthday.*

> result   condition
>
> *We would have greener surroundings if we lived in a rainy climate.*

2. Conditional sentences indicate real and hypothetical, untrue, situations. The verb tense in each clause shows whether the situation is real or hypothetical.

Real or Factual Conditionals in the Present or Future

In real conditionals, which are about real ideas or situations in the present or future, the simple present is used in the *if* clause. The verb tense in the result clause is the simple present or future, depending on the idea or situation.

- For habitual actions or situations, use the simple present in the result clause.

> *If I* **don't write** *my shopping list down, I always* **forget** *something at the store.*

- For a predictable fact or general truth, use either the simple present or the simple future in the result clause.

> *If it* **rains,** *the company usually* **postpones** *the picnic.*

> *If the temperature* **falls** *below 32°F, the roads* **will freeze.**

NOTE: When or *whenever* can replace *if* in conditional sentences that express habitual actions, predictable facts, or general truths.

> *My family loves to have a fire in the fireplace* **whenever** *it rains.*

> **When** *it snows hard, the schools close.*

> **When** *the temperature rises above 32°F, the snow will melt.*

- To express an action or situation in the future, use the simple future in the result clause.

> *If I* **don't wake up** *early tomorrow, I* **will be late** *for work again.*

- To express ideas like ability, necessity, possibility, or predictions in a conditional sentence, use modals or phrasal modals in the result clause.

> *If it* **rains,** *we* **should cancel** *the picnic.*

> *The plane* **won't be able** *to take off, if the storm* **continues.**

Hypothetical Conditionals in the Present or Future

- To write about hypothetical, imaginary, or impossible situations in the present or future, use the simple past in the *if* clause and *would* + the base form of the verb in the result clause. *Could* can also be used in the result clause to express a possibility.

    *If my parents **were** here, they **would help** us.*

    (In truth, my parents are not here, so they cannot help us.)

    *If Maylin **had** a million dollars, she **would quit** her job.*

    (In truth, Maylin doesn't have a million dollars, so she won't quit her job.)

    *If Maylin **had** a million dollars, she **could quit** her job.* (could = would be able to)

NOTE: *Were* is used for both singular and plural subjects in formal writing. *Was* can be used informally, but it is not considered the best choice for formal writing.

    *If she **were** a little taller, she **would be** taller than her father.*

- Hypothetical conditionals can also be used to make suggestions. In the following example, the writer is suggesting that the listener work less so that he or she can spend more time studying.

    *If I **were** you, I **would study** more and **work** less.*

Hypothetical Conditionals in the Past

- To write about hypothetical, imaginary, or impossible situations in the past, use the past perfect in the *if* clause and *would* + *have* + past participle in the result clause. The situations in these conditional sentences did not happen. *Would* expresses a desired or predictable result. *Could* and *might* can also be used in the result clause to express a possibility.

    *If Tao **had graduated** last June, he **would have moved** to Beijing.*

    (Tao didn't graduate in June, so he didn't move.)

    *If I **hadn't been late** for the interview, I **could have gotten** the job.*

    (could have gotten = would have been able to get)

Mixed-Time Hypothetical Conditionals

- Use a mixed-time hypothetical conditional to write about an untrue condition in the past with an untrue result in the present.

    past perfect   would + verb

    If Lani had written a best-selling novel, she would be famous now.

    (She didn't write a best-selling novel in the past, so she is not famous now.)

- Use a mixed-time hypothetical conditional to write about an untrue condition in the present with an untrue result in the past.

    simple past   would + have + past participle

    If I had a car, I would have taken you to school.

    (I don't have a car now, so I couldn't have taken you to school in the past.)

3. The subordinating conjunction *unless* means *if . . . not.*

>We will live in Barcelona **unless** our plans change.

(We will live in Barcelona if our plans do not change.)

>I always finish my homework **unless** I am interrupted by my little sister.

(I always finish my homework if I am not interrupted by my little sister.)

4. The subordinating conjunctions *whether or not* and *even if* mean the condition does not affect the result.

result	condition

>*Adrian is going to change her major whether or not her parents agree.*

(Adrian will change her major. Her parents' opinion will not influence her decision.)

condition	result

>*Even if we are not finished, we have to turn in the test in one hour.*

(We have to turn in the test in one hour. It doesn't matter if we finish or not.)

5. Modals other than *would* are frequently used in conditional sentences. They express meanings such as advice, prediction, ability, and possibility.

Advice: *If you fly a long distance, you* **should try** *to drink a lot of water.*

Prediction: *If roses are planted in the winter,* **they should bloom** *the following spring.*

Ability: *If we practiced more, we* **could speak** *Spanish better.*

Possibility: *If Sasha had practiced more, she* **might have been** *a concert cellist.*

6. Sentences that follow conditionals may mention additional results. In most cases, these results require the use of a modal such as *would* or *could.*

>*If Mary Ann got financial support, she would go to dental school. She* **would like** *to be a dentist so that she* **could help** *low-income children improve their dental health.*

WRITING TIP

Scan your writing for the subordinating conjunctions *if, unless,* and *even if.* When you see one of these words, circle it, and review the rules for conditional sentences. Check that the verb phrase is correct in both clauses.

Self Check

Circle the sentence that uses conditional sentences correctly.

1. (a) Lyra will be on time for class if she drives to school.

  (b) Lyra would be on time for class if she drives to school.

2. (a) If Mrs. Candelaria taught the class again, she would assign fewer essays. She would also do a few other things differently.

  (b) If Mrs. Candelaria taught the class again, she would assign fewer essays. She will also do a few other things differently.

3. (a) If Julie had been invited to go horseback riding after class yesterday, she would have gone.

  (b) If Julie were invited to go horseback riding after class yesterday, she would have gone.

4. (a) If I was you, I would buy a new car.

  (b) If I were you, I would buy a new car.

5. (a) Mr. Gupta would have bought the shoes now if he had gotten the discount coupon.

  (b) Mr. Gupta would buy the shoes now if he had gotten the discount coupon.

EDITING PRACTICE

1. *Put a check (✓) next to the sentences that use conditionals correctly. Correct the sentences that have errors in structure and/or meaning.*

_____ **1.** It would hurt Rudy's feelings if his friends tell secrets about him.

_____ **2.** If I were the queen of England, I would wear a crown of diamonds.

_____ **3.** When children will wait patiently, they get what they want.

_____ **4.** If Mr. Canon had a pet, he would be happier than he is now because he will have companionship.

_____ **5.** Traditions are difficult to maintain. If people don't keep their families together.

_____ **6.** Dr. Ashcroft would be my favorite professor, if he had given me an A on the term paper.

_____ **7.** We go out to dinner unless my mother wants to cook.

_____ **8.** If parents communicated well with their children, both parents and children will be happy and feel better about each other.

_____ **9.** Mrs. Steele would be a school principal if she had received the right credentials.

_____ **10.** If Bernice goes to the concert, she would hear a lot of songs that she knows.

_____ **11.** If my car insurance had gone down, I could have bought a new car.

_____ **12.** Congress is going to raise taxes even if the voters are against it.

2. *Read the following paragraph. Complete the paragraph with the correct choice in each conditional sentence.*

As an urban planning student, someday I hope to make life easier

for people living in metropolitan areas by improving parklands, public

transportation, and community meeting areas. If I designed an ideal city,

I _____ on these three important aspects
        1. would focus / will focus

of city life. If it _____ possible, the city
                    2. was / were

would have a lot of open land for hiking, fishing, picnicking, and other

outdoor activities. The city laws _____
                                  3. will mandate / would mandate

that this land could never be developed. If the city were large, I

_____ a safe and efficient subway
        4. would design / had designed

system. This system _____
                    5. will be / would be

underground and nonpolluting. I would also spend a great deal

of time designing fun and educational community areas that

_____ all citizens from the youngest
        6. attract / would attract

to the oldest. If the city _____ money
                          7. had / has

to spend on community meeting areas, I would like to see museums,

schools, and parks that host concerts and classes. In all cities, if people

have parks, safe and efficient public transportation, and a feeling of

community, they _____ content.
                8. will be / would be

Urban planners know this now, but if they had realized it earlier,

we _____ as many urban problems
        9. would not have had / would not have

today. It is my dream to create peaceful cities and happy citizens. If I

_____ on time, I will be able to begin my
        10. graduated / graduate

dream in two years.

3. *In the following paragraph, five of the underlined verbs have errors. Write the correct conditional form above each of the five verbs with errors.*

If I faced a life-threatening challenge, I would make some changes in my
        1   2

life. First, if I were about to die, I will review my life. If I have the time and
            3   4   5

opportunity, I would travel around the world. I would probably want to do
                    6   7

as many things as I could because I would not have much time left on Earth.
                                        8

If I had a disease that can harm other people, I will have to stay away from
   9   10   11

public places. When I looked back on my life, I would see if there were any
                                                12   13

bad deeds that I had done and I would try to make up for them. Fortunately, I

am not facing a life-threatening challenge, but the thought of this has made

me evaluate my life and how I am living it. If I realize that I am making
                                                14

mistakes now, I change my behavior before it is too late.
                15

4. *The following paragraph has ten errors in the use of conditional sentences. Find and correct the errors.*

If you wanted to save money and
gain peace in your life, you should try
planting a vegetable garden. Saving
money and gaining peace may seem
unrelated, but both are achievable by
planting a garden. If you are familiar
with the inexpensive price of seeds, you
understood that it is economical to grow
a vegetable garden. If you have found joy in growing a plant, you know that

it is possible to find peace in planting. Keep these two ideas in mind as you

gather a few things that you need before you begin your garden. If you had

a small area of land, it will be easy to begin your garden; however, a lot of land isn't necessary. You succeed even if you have only a small patio with a few containers. First, it is important to have good soil. If you composted your garbage, you already have the perfect fertilizer for your garden. If you don't compost, it is possible to find good fertilizers at any nursery. Next, it's time to decide which vegetables to plant. This depends on the time of year. If it was the cool season, vegetables such as broccoli, lettuce, and onions will do well. Summer vegetables like tomatoes, cucumbers, and corn would grow well if it's warm outside. Depending on the plant, you may begin harvesting in as soon as four weeks. One downside of gardening is pests. Whenever you had planted your vegetables, you will have to be aware of vegetable-eating bugs. Try planting a vegetable garden any time of year, and see what you save financially and gain emotionally. Hopefully, at some point in the future you will say to yourself, "If only I had known the benefits of a vegetable garden earlier, I would save so much money and find enjoyment so much sooner."

WRITING TOPICS

Study the student paragraph that uses conditional sentences. Underline all the examples of conditional forms that you find in this paragraph.

Most academic paragraphs, whether they are part of an essay or stand alone, include a clear topic sentence, a body, and a concluding sentence. Notice that this paragraph has these three important parts of an academic paragraph. Use this paragraph as a model when you write about one of the topics below.

Language teachers have many suggestions for the best way to learn a foreign language. If I were a language teacher, I would tell my students to live or travel to the country where the language is spoken. By living with the language, students naturally learn it. First of all, my students would hear the language every day. If they went shopping, rode public transportation, or visited tourist sights, they would be exposed to the language in natural settings. This would be helpful for learning vocabulary and improving pronunciation. Living in the country would also help my students develop an appreciation of the country's culture. If someone enjoys the history, people, and customs of a country, the language becomes much easier to learn. Living in the country allows language learners to see and experience the richness of the place and people. Lastly, learning a language while living in the country would let my students learn as if they were babies. Just like babies, my students would ask the names of unfamiliar items, and they would learn the answers in a relaxed environment. Sometimes learning a language in a classroom can be stressful. Learning like babies who are slowly introduced to new vocabulary, grammar, and sounds would make my students successful language learners. Learning a new language is a long process, but living in a foreign country with the language makes it an adventure.

Choose one of the topics below and write at least one paragraph. Be sure to use conditional sentences. After you complete your first draft, concentrate on editing your work. Keep in mind the editing practice from this chapter.

1. Describe one problem that exists in the world today. The problem can be a global or regional one. If you could solve this problem, how would you do it? If you solved the problem, how would the world or life change? If this problem had never existed, how would our world or lives have been different?

2. Because you have been studying the English language for many years, you probably have opinions on the best way to learn a new language. If someone wanted to learn your first language, how would you teach him or her? What techniques did you find helpful while learning English that you would use as a teacher of your language? What could someone learn about the customs and culture of your country if you taught them your native language?

Go to page 156 for more practice with conditionals.

Prepositions

GRAMMAR FOCUS

At this point in your study of English, you are familiar with many prepositions. However, you may still need practice with these because prepositions frequently change meaning and are often used idiomatically. An incorrectly chosen preposition may confuse your readers and convey the wrong meaning. For example, the prepositions in the following two sentences change the meaning of the verb.

Leila cares **about** eliminating worldwide hunger.	Leila thinks this is important and she is interested in it.
Caden cares **for** his elderly grandmother.	Caden looks after his grandmother because she cannot do many things for herself.

In this chapter, you will review the basic meanings of commonly used prepositions and get additional practice with preposition + adjective and preposition + verb combinations.

Pretest

Check your understanding of prepositions. Put a check (✓) next to the sentences that are correct.

____ **1.** We go to school in Running Springs College.

____ **2.** The Simpsons have been on vacation since two weeks.

____ **3.** The shoe repair shop is besides the market.

____ **4.** The research assignment is due on March 11.

____ **5.** Babies are dependent of their parents.

____ **6.** Asha was so proud herself when she graduated with a 4.0 GPA.

____ **7.** They read about Stonehenge in their archaeology course.

____ **8.** The childcare center is on campus.

____ **9.** The children wait for the school bus every morning.

____ **10.** Many small businesses begin in homes and eventually move to larger locations.

The following paragraph uses many prepositions that you will study in this chapter. As you circle the sixteen prepositions in the paragraph, notice how some of these prepositions occur together with certain verbs and adjectives. Some prepositions also show place and time. Use the prepositions from this paragraph to complete the exercise below.

The United States Postal Service has an interesting history that includes some amazing statistics. The original postal service was established by Benjamin Franklin in 1775 in Philadelphia. In 1983, the U.S. Postal Service became an independent organization that does not rely on taxpayer dollars for support. It has recently had to cut costs because of the increase in e-mail usage and competitors such as Federal Express and UPS. The U.S. Postal Service is the second largest private employer in the United States and has the largest number of nonmilitary vehicles in the world. It delivers approximately 177 billion pieces of mail every year. The average American citizen may take mail delivery for granted, but when one looks at the size and responsibility of this organization, we should all be appreciative of its speed and accuracy.

verb + preposition

1. rely _____

2. look _____

3. take something _____ granted

adjective + preposition

1. be appreciative _____

prepositions of place and time

1. in _____ (a city)

2. in _____ (a country)

3. in _____ (a year)

4. _____ the world

PREPOSITIONS

A preposition connects a noun or a pronoun to the rest of a sentence and indicates a relationship such as time, place, or position. Prepositions are usually one word but can also be two or more words. The most frequently used one-word prepositions are *at, by, for, from, in, of, on, to,* and *with*. Some prepositions with more than one word are *according to, along with, away from,* and *in front of*. The following section provides guidelines that can assist you in using the correct prepositions.

Types of Prepositions

1. Prepositions of time

The prepositions of time include:

Month/year	**in**	Aidan arrived **in** June. He arrived *in* 2007.
Day/date	**on**	He began classes **on** Monday. He began class **on** June 5.
Specific time	**at**	The classes started **at** 9:00 A.M.
	by	We will be there **by** 6:00 P.M. / Tuesday / November 3.
	from . . . to	Most businesses are open **from** 8:00 A.M. **to** 5:00 P.M.
	since	Ms. Figueroa has been here **since** 9:00 A.M. / Tuesday / June / 2009.
	until	She waited for him **until** 11:00 A.M. / Saturday / October / last year.
General time	**before**	She left **before** lunch.
	after	I am leaving **after** the exam.
Approximate time	**about**	I'll be home **about** 2:00 P.M.
	around	Let's meet **around** 5:00 P.M.
	between . . . and	He said he'll call **between** nine **and** ten o'clock.
Duration	**for**	My family lived in Guam **for** six years.
	through	I have thought of you often **through** the years.
	during	We ate a lot of popcorn **during** the movie.

WRITING TIP

In academic writing *until* is a better choice than *till*. In spoken English, *until* is reduced to *till*, but this is not acceptable in formal written English.

2. Prepositions of place or position

The prepositions of place include:

City/country	in	Fred lived **in** Toronto for three years. He lived **in** Canada for five years.
Street	on	He worked **on** Battery Street.
Address	at	He lives **at** 16 Queen Lane.
Motion	to	He goes **to** the park for lunch. *(walk to, run to, drive to, ride to, race to, fly to)*
	toward	They walked **toward** me.
In a direction	past	Charlotte and I drove **past** the hospital.
Position	at	Let's meet **at** the library.
	beside	The dog is sitting **beside** its owner.
	between	My house is **between** the park and the fire station.
	in	The lecture notes are **in** this notebook.
	on	The book is **on** the desk.

Some other prepositions that commonly show position are *against, along, beneath, beyond, down, outside,* and *up*.

3. Prepositions of manner

The prepositions of manner tell how something is done. They include:

at	She is good **at** speaking in front of large groups.
with	They finished the test **with** difficulty.
by	He can understand their accent **by** listening carefully.
on	I like to travel **on** airplanes.

4. Prepositions of comparison

The prepositions of comparison include:

as . . . as	The storm made the sky **as** dark **as** night.
like	We are so close that he is **like** my brother.
unlike	Honolulu is **unlike** the other cities on Oahu.

5. Preposition of possession

The preposition of possession includes:

of	Dino is a good friend **of** mine. He wrote a book **of** poems.

NOTE: Use an apostrophe + s, not the preposition *of*, to show possession with living things.

> Our neighbor**'s** house is very large.

> The dog**'s** tail is always wagging.

Self Check 1

Circle the sentence that uses the correct preposition.

1. **(a)** The passport office is at Westwood Boulevard.

   (b) The passport office is on Westwood Boulevard.

2. **(a)** The movie starts at six o'clock.

   (b) The movie starts on six o'clock.

3. **(a)** We arrived to Malaysia at May.

   (b) We arrived in Malaysia in May.

4. **(a)** Ariana looks like her mother. They could be sisters.

   (b) Ariana looks of her mother. They could be sisters.

5. **(a)** It's easiest to get downtown by train.

   (b) It's easiest to get downtown in train.

Adjective + Preposition Combinations

Prepositions are frequently combined with adjectives, for example *good at* and *interested in*. As you write, refer to the following short list of ten commonly used adjective + preposition combinations and to the longer list in Appendix 5. Notice how the following sentences use a stative verb such as *be, feel, look,* or *seem* then the adjective + preposition combination.

> The class is **concerned about** *final exams.*

> Yi Ting looks **similar to** *her sister.*

> Tourists feel **nervous about** *earthquakes when they are in California.*

| afraid of | dependent on | excited about | proud of | sorry for/about |
| capable of | different from | full of | ready for | worried about |

Verb + Preposition Combinations

Prepositions are frequently combined with verbs, for example *believe in* and *belong to*. As you write, refer to the following short list of twelve commonly used verb + preposition combinations and to the longer list in Appendix 5. Notice how the following sentences use verb + preposition combinations.

> *I **forgot about** my doctor's appointment.*
>
> *The English Department **insists on** in-class writing exams.*
>
> *Professor Johnson **is talking to** Han about his grade in the class.*

agree with	feel like	know about	read about
decide on	graduate from	plan on	take care of
depend on	hear about/of something	prepare for	wait for

WRITING TIP

Check an ESL or learner's dictionary under the adjective or verb for additional adjective + preposition and verb + preposition combinations.

Self Check 2

Circle the sentence that uses the correct adjective + preposition or verb + preposition combination.

1. (a) Memorial Day is different from Veteran's Day.

(b) Memorial Day is different than Veteran's Day.

2. (a) Many successful businessmen never graduate from college.

(b) Many successful businessmen never graduate at college.

3. (a) Retail businesses are preparing about the holiday shopping season.

(b) Retail businesses are preparing for the holiday shopping season.

4. (a) Parents are proud of their children.

(b) Parents proud of their children.

5. (a) We depend to the Internet for everything nowadays.

(b) We depend on the Internet for everything nowadays.

WRITING TIP

To help remember common adjective + preposition and verb + preposition combinations, begin a list of the combinations that you use frequently or that you've made mistakes with in the past. By creating your own personal list, you will begin to learn the correct preposition combinations that you need in your writing.

IDIOMATIC EXPRESSIONS WITH PREPOSITIONS

Idiomatic expressions with prepositions are set phrases whose prepositions and word order cannot be changed. Like many expressions with prepositions, you may have to memorize these.

Expressions of Location

at home/work/the office:	*We'll be* **at home** *until five o'clock.*
at school/church:	*Chen and Bao are* **at school** *today.*
in bed:	*Maggie was still* **in bed** *at noon.*
on campus:	*Most freshmen live* **on campus**.
on the Internet:	*It's easy to find a lot of information* **on the Internet**.

Expressions of Time

at night:	*Some people find it difficult to drive* **at night**.
in the morning/afternoon/evening:	*The package is supposed to arrive* **in the afternoon**.
on time:	*The Washington, D.C., to New York flight is* **on time**.

Expressions of Manner

by train/bus/airplane:	*It is quickest to travel long distances* **by airplane**.
on television:	*My favorite show is* **on television** *every Monday night.*

WRITING TIP

One of the best ways to improve your vocabulary and use of prepositions is to read. By reading English newspapers, magazines, and books, you will become familiar with the correct usage of common words and phrases.

Self Check 3

Circle the sentence that uses the correct idiomatic expression with a preposition.

1. (a) People who are night owls have trouble waking up at the morning.

   (b) People who are night owls have trouble waking up in the morning.

2. (a) Lucca was so sick that he spent the whole day in bed.

   (b) Lucca was so sick that he spent the whole day on bed.

3. (a) Many youth organizations meet at church during the week.

   (b) Many youth organizations meet to church during the week.

4. (a) Most soap operas are on television at the afternoon.

   (b) Most soap operas are on television in the afternoon.

5. (a) They have to finish the assignment by time because the teacher won't accept late work.

   (b) They have to finish the assignment on time because the teacher won't accept late work.

EDITING PRACTICE

1. *Put a check (✓) next to the sentences that use prepositions correctly. Correct the sentences that have errors.*

_____ **1.** Kodak dominated the photography industry from the late 1800s to the early 2000s.

_____ **2.** The rain has not stopped since two days.

_____ **3.** Children who are under ten years old are often afraid by the dark.

_____ **4.** High school seniors wait at their college acceptance letters every spring.

_____ **5.** I love Chinese food. I feel like sizzling rice soup for dinner tonight.

_____ **6.** The president of the United States lives on 1600 Pennsylvania Avenue.

_____ **7.** Honda is capable of manufacturing 4 million vehicles per year.

_____ **8.** The Cho family is excited their upcoming trip to Rome.

_____ **9.** He finally decided the blue car instead of the red one.

_____ **10.** The mail usually arrives between two to three o'clock in the afternoon.

_____ **11.** Chloe depends for her tutor for help in math.

_____ **12.** Mr. Penny has been at the office seven days a week for over a month.

2. *Read the following paragraph. Complete the paragraph with the correct prepositions.*

A nickname has traditionally been an informal name given by a friend

or family member that shows how someone is different _____
                                                        1. from / than

others. For example, if someone is good _____ running
                                         2. in / at

fast, she may have been nicknamed *Speedy,* or if someone is interested

_____ dancing, she could have been called *Twinkle Toes.*
3. in /on

Nicknames slowly fell out of fashion but have become popular again

_____ the Internet. People rarely use their real names on blogs
4. in / on

or social networking sites because they are concerned _____
                                                       5. on / about

privacy. The nicknames that are used on electronic media must be

_____ other common nicknames because unique names are the
6. unlike / about

only way to distinguish one person from the next when we cannot see or talk

to them in person. For people who cannot think of their own nicknames, they

might have heard _____ nickname generators that will create
7. about / on

a nickname for them. Similar _____ traditional and Internet
8. to / for

nicknames, we know _____ company nicknames such as Bud
9. for / about

for Budweiser and T-bird for the Ford Thunderbird. These nicknames have

become so common that consumers might have forgotten _____
10. about / by

the original name. Like a company's nickname, a person's nickname should

be chosen carefully because it may become more popular than one's given

name.

3. *In the following paragraph, the underlined prepositions are not correct. Write the correct preposition above each underlined error.*

The history of the biggest retailer in the world, Wal-Mart, began <u>on</u>
1

1940. This was when Sam Walton got a job at J.C. Penney <u>at</u> Arkansas. <u>In</u>
2   3

May 9, 1950, Walton opened his first store, Walton's 5 & 10 in Bentonville,

Arkansas. Walton's 5 & 10 grew <u>for</u> keeping its prices lower than its
4

competitors' prices. As the number of Sam Walton's stores grew, his goal was

for his stores to be just <u>for</u> other discount chains but more successful. He
5

quickly succeeded by following this model, and <u>on</u> 1967, the chain had
6

grown to twenty-seven stores and changed its name to Wal-Mart. <u>For</u> 1967
7

to today, Wal-Mart has grown to over 6,000 stores worldwide and more than

$300 billion in annual sales. Even with Wal-Mart's success at keeping its prices

low, its huge size and business practices concern many people. They are

primarily worried <u>of</u> the low wages <u>by</u> Wal-Mart employees. Though there
8   9

have been thousands of lawsuits against Wal-Mart, the company has become

such an icon that the original Walton's 5 & 10 <u>on</u> 105 North Main Street in

10

Bentonville, Arkansas, is now the Wal-Mart Visitor Center, which hosts

thousands of visitors every year who want to know the Wal-Mart story.

4. *The following paragraph has ten errors in the use of prepositions. Find and correct the errors.*

Many environmental activists are concerned of the state of the world's fish population. They see overfishing as a major problem that will eventually affect everyone on the planet. Overfishing occurs when fishermen catch so many fish that the remaining fish are not capable in breeding to

replace themselves. This is a problem for millions of people worldwide

who depend for the oceans for their livelihood and primary source of food.

Additionally, it is a problem for the rest of the earth's people who may not

have a direct relationship with the ocean but whose lives are still dependent

by healthy oceans and fish populations. One way to take care about the fish

population is to improve current fishing methods. Bottom trawling and

fishing with huge nets result in fishing boats that are full in marine life that

the fishermen don't want or use. This dead sea life is simply thrown back into

the ocean. In addition to stopping wasteful fishing methods, average people

should educate themselves about this topic by reading for the best types of

fish to eat and how to decrease overfishing in their local communities. If we don't do this soon, many scientists are afraid for losing entire fish species within the next twenty-five years. Rather than waiting about fish to disappear from our oceans, we must insist for changing the current fishing methods and educating the world's people about this problem.

WRITING TOPICS

Study the prepositions in this student paragraph. Underline some examples of adjective + preposition and verb + preposition combinations. Also underline other types of prepositions that you studied about at the beginning of this chapter.

Most academic paragraphs, whether they are part of an essay or stand alone, include a clear topic sentence, a body, and a concluding sentence. Notice that this paragraph has these three important parts of an academic paragraph. Use this paragraph as a model when you write about one of the topics below.

In most countries throughout the world, the average age of marriage has risen for the past 100 years. There are two main reasons for this trend. Industrialization is the first one. The more advanced a country becomes, the longer its people wait to get married. Industrialization leads to more women in the workforce, which naturally results in marriages at an older age. Industrialization also increases the need for education, so people stay in school for longer periods of time. The other reason for the rise in the age of marriage is feminism. During the past several decades, women have become aware of their rights and their potential without a husband. These changes have been good for society, but some countries are nervous about this trend because later marriages result in fewer babies being born. If a country's population doesn't grow, its economy will shrink. Although most countries hope for industrialization, a highly educated population, and a strong workforce, they also worry about the long-term consequences of these advances.

Choose one of the topics below and write at least one paragraph. Be sure to use some of the prepositions that you studied in this chapter. After you complete your first draft, concentrate on editing your work. Keep in mind the editing practice from this chapter.

1. In many parts of the world, couples are getting married much later in life than they did a few decades ago. Why do you think this is happening? What are some of the results of later marriages?

2. Raising a family can be compared to caring for a garden. What must people do to have both a healthy family and a healthy garden?

Go to page 159 for more practice with prepositions.

Extra Editing Practice

EDITING FOCUS

Use the following pieces of writing to practice editing for grammar points that you have focused on in the previous chapters. When you edit your own writing, it is important to look for a variety of grammatical errors; therefore, each exercise in this chapter requires that you edit for more than one type of grammatical structure.

> **WRITING TIP**
>
> Don't forget to schedule editing time into the time you plan for writing your essays. Careful editing requires at least 10 percent of your writing time. If it takes five hours to write an essay, plan to spend at least another thirty minutes editing your writing.

TENSES, MODALS, AND PASSIVE VOICE

1. *Edit carefully for errors in verb tenses, modals, and the passive voice. There are ten errors in the following paragraph.*

It is interesting to see how unexpected life events caused people to [*cause*] change and grow. My grandmother is a good example of someone who had unanticipated events change the course of her life and her outlook. She was born during World War I and was raise [*ed*] in a traditional family where the father went to work and the mother had stayed home to take care of the children. She believed that her life will follow [*would*] the same course. She married early and had three children before the age of twenty-three. Unfortunately, one was died before his first birthday. World War II was the second unexpected event to change the life she had planned for herself. Her husband was send to [*sent*] Europe and killed in France. Before his death, my grandmother had taken evening courses at a local college. She eventually was received her master's degree in social work and worked for the state for thirty years. Because her life didn't follow the path she had planned, she has become a flexible, open-minded person. Unlike many people her age, she accepts modern ideas about marriage, divorce, religion, and pregnancy. She knows from experience that life is unpredictable and the world will continues to move forward. From her I have learned that we should not have been too rigid or we are disappointed about our lives.

be   we will be.

TENSES, COORDINATION, AND PARALLEL STRUCTURE

2. *Edit carefully for errors in verb tenses, coordination, and parallel structure. There are ten errors in the following paragraph.*

Should I live at home and commute to campus or should I move into the on-campus dormitory? This question runs through the minds of many students as they prepared to enter college. There are definitely benefits to both living situations. Many parents encourage their children to live on campus so they can experience freedom, friendship, and the responsible of being on their own. Other parents encourage their children to live on campus so that they learn to fully appreciate home but all of its comforts. On the other hand, many parents prefer that their college-age children commute. This option costs less money, keeps children under the parents' control, and students have more time to study and less time to worry about cooking, cleaning, and laundry.

When I made this decision, there were several factors that influence me to live on campus rather than commuting from home. I knew one of the advantages will be meeting other students easily. Other factors that influenced me were the convenience of not having to hunt for a parking space each morning and not having to wake up early to drive to school. I have a good friend who lives very close to campus, yet he commutes every day. Not only

he has breakfast prepared for him every morning, but he also has a lot of

spending money because he isn't paying dorm fees. However, he has made

fewer new friends, and he doesn't attend as many parties as I do. Overall, no

living situation was perfect. When students make decisions about where they

will live the next year, they should realize that there will be both positive and

negative aspects to any choice they make.

MODALS, NOUNS, AND DETERMINERS

3. *Edit carefully for errors in the use of modals, nouns, and determiners. There are ten errors in the following paragraph.*

All communications skills are important, but I believe

the most important of these skills is writing well. This skill

seems to be necessary in all parts of modern life. With so

many communication in writing, I find that I judge the other
much

people by the way that they write. Clothing and speech may

has communicated the first impression in the past, but today,
have   *a*

writing may be the only contact we have with other people.

I have recently learned the importances of writing in the

business world. I have gone on several job interviews and at

each one, I was asked to write the short essay. Many employers
a

are looking for people who are able to write well. Therefore,

grammar is important for students. When I was in high school, I didn't realize
The

an importance of grammar, and my grades suffered because my teachers
The

shouldn't clearly understand the ideas in my writing. I eventually learned
couldn't

to use good grammar and a clear writing style. Same lessons can be applied when writing letters, sending e-mail, and jotting notes to family and friends. Because we may be evaluated by colleagues, peers, family, or friends on our written words, good grammars and writing skills are necessary.

grammar

TENSES, PASSIVE VOICE, AND ADJECTIVE CLAUSES

4. *Edit carefully for errors in the use of verb tenses, passive voice, and adjective clauses. There are ten errors in the following paragraph.*

In London, England, there are many activities and sights that they are educational as well as fun. Some fun, educational sights included the British Museum, the National Gallery, and the Tower of London. The British Museum, that is one of the busiest tourist attractions in the city, has a large collection that may require several days to

see. At the National Gallery, some tours are guide by volunteers to help guests see the sizable collection. Before it became a busy tourist attraction, the Tower of London has a history that people today finds horrible yet fascinating. Some activities in London that is fun but also educational include wandering around Soho, shopping at a Sunday morning street market, and dining at popular London restaurants. When one was in a foreign country, it's always interesting to watch people have a different culture, language, or outlook. Even though these activities are not consider educational in the traditional sense, they still teach us lessons about the world.

MODALS, VERB FORMS, AND GERUNDS AND INFINITIVES

5. *Edit carefully for errors in modals, verb forms, and gerunds and infinitives. There are ten errors in the following paragraph. There may be more than one way to correct some errors.*

Peer pressure has became a common problem for many high school students over the past several decades. Many teenagers feel they might not say no to their friends because acceptance is very important at this time in their lives. Sometimes peer pressure can be positive and other times it can be negative. A lot of adolescents make their friends to begin smoking, drinking, cutting school, and driving too fast. In contrast, a student may decides to study, play sports, and joining academic clubs because of positive peer pressure. During the transition from junior high to high school, I saw the best student change to the worst student due to the bad influences of his peers. As a young adult, I now enjoy to think about the many good influences in high school that helped me continuing my education. Because I was fortunate to have positive role models during my teenage years, in the future I plan help teenagers who are facing many negative influences and are thinking about give in to negative peer pressure. I believe that when a teenager has one positive role model, it has to mean the difference between success and failure. For this reason, I hope to make a positive difference in some teenage lives.

COORDINATION, PARALLEL STRUCTURE, CONDITIONALS, AND ADVERB CLAUSES

6. *Edit carefully for errors in the use of coordination, parallel structure, and conditional sentences. There are ten errors in the following paragraph.*

All Isaac and Juliet can think about is a vacation, even though they just graduated from college and started working three months ago. Both of them love their jobs, but they can't believe they won't have a vacation for another nine months. They said that if they had known the company's vacation policy before starting the job, they would negotiate for time off at six months rather than twelve. This will make their first summer without a vacation easier. At this point, all they can do is dream of time off from work. If Isaac takes a vacation now, he would go to some remote location without any distractions from meetings, phones, and receiving e-mail. He would hike, read, relax, and truly appreciate his few days away from work. Juliet, on the other hand, would travel to a place with a lot of people and excitement if she goes on a vacation. She will like to go to a big city with shopping, fine dining, and dances. In reality, Isaac nor Juliet has a vacation day in the near future. They tell their friends who are still in school to appreciate the generous amount of time off they have as students. When their friends go on vacation, Neither Isaac nor Juliet wants to hear about it! If Isaac and Juliet were back in school, they would have enjoyed each and every day they were not in class. Neither of them realized the importance of vacations until three months ago.

ADVERB CLAUSES AND CONDITIONALS

7. *Edit carefully for errors in the use of adverb clauses and conditional sentences. There are ten errors in the following paragraph.*

According to Michael Korda in his book *Success!*, "success is relative." In other words, what one person considers a success another may consider a failure. To be successful, people have to define the word for themselves in order they know when they have achieved success. Korda says that not everyone wants to run a corporation or lead a country, and it may be problematic to start with so grand expectations that are likely to fail. In fact, an unattainable goal leads to laziness because the goal is beyond one's capabilities. Korda suggests that where we set a goal, the goal should be reasonably realistic. After we make a habit of succeeding with moderate goals it's easier to achieve success with larger ones. If one had made success a habit, achieving bigger goals becomes natural and realistic.

Although Michael Korda makes a good point about making success a habit, but I believe it is always important to dream big. If I had listened to his advice earlier, I might not start college. Because no one in my family had ever gone to college before, I didn't think I was capable of doing college work. However, I had teachers, counselors, and friends who encouraged me. Because their encouragement, I have just finished my second year at a university. If people asked me for advice on success, I would tell them the opposite of Korda's advice. I will encourage them to set their goals as big as possible. They might not achieve their top goal, but if they don't dream big, they may not have accomplished smaller goals on the way to their top goal.

WORD FORMS, COMPARATIVES AND SUPERLATIVES, AND VERB FORMS

8. *Edit carefully for errors in word forms, comparatives and superlatives, and verb forms. There are ten errors in the following paragraph.*

There are some importance rules that people must to follow when they use e-mail. These rules are called netiquette because they are etiquette rules for the Internet. The importantest rules are the following. First, people should never get anger on e-mail. It is better to have a discuss face-to-face than on the computer. Another good rule is to edit all messages carefully before they are sent. Nobody enjoys to get messages full of misspelled words and grammar errors. People consider writing in all capital letters being like yelling. Therefore, the last netiquette rule is to follow all capitalization rules. These e-mail rules are so important that many companies have classes on netiquette. Businesses want their employees use e-mail correctly. There are even many popular books on the topic of netiquette. Now that computers and the Internet are commoner than face-to-face communication, everyone has to learn a new set of rules for to be polite.

APPENDIX 1: PRACTICE WITH AUTHENTIC LANGUAGE

CHAPTER 1 Tenses and Time Shifts

Read the following selection from The Daily Pilot, *a local newspaper from southern California. Choose the correct verb tense.*

Biking the Distance

by Tom Ragen

Salome Hernandez doesn't use high-tech gear. . . . He's just got his 20-gear

Trek road bike and a helmet.

Hernandez pedals to his job at Muldoon's Irish Pub, where he

_____ as a busboy[1] for more than two decades.
     1. has been working / works

He _____ back and forth to the job for 22 years,
     2. is riding / has been riding

earning minimum wage, plus tips, bringing in $2,200 a month during the good

years.

But he's no boy.

He's a 52-year-old man who _____ the
     3. is knowing / knows

value of holding a job, having grown up in an impoverished part of rural Mexico.

He's an immigrant who _____ roots in the United
     4. established / has established

States more than two decades ago and _____
     5. doesn't look back / hasn't looked back

since then, except for an occasional visit home during the holidays. . . .

"I love my job," said Hernandez as he nervously watched plates fill up at

nearby tables while he _____ a few questions. "All
     6. had answered / was answering

the customers like me, and that's a good reason to come to work. That's the best

reason."

....
[1] **busboy** person in restaurant who removes dirty dishes from tables

....

Some of those customers sometimes offer him rides when the weather turns stormy.

Other times the wait staff at the pub pulls him aside and says, "Enough is enough. Let us drive you home in this rain."

Hernandez often _____. It's more fun
                    7. refuses / refused
being independent, he said. "I love biking. I do it for the fresh air, for my health," said Hernandez, who was born in the small town of Ezequiel Montes, in the Mexican state of Queretaro.

He looks pretty fit because of all the pedaling.

Hernandez isn't just supporting himself financially. He

_____ his two daughters on his busboy wages:
    8. is supporting / will be supporting
21-year-old Andrea, who attends college, and Heidi, 25.

"They both _____ for jobs, but I'm here
                9. look / are looking
for them until they figure out what they want to do with their lives," he said. "It's important that they get an education first. That's the most important thing."

Sometimes, Hernandez added, family finances can be somewhat of a struggle.

"When the economy is bad, like it _____
                                    10. is / has been
lately, and there aren't as many customers, it can be really difficult," he said.

But he's always got his bike, he said.

"Sometimes, it can be a relief just pedaling away," he added. "Sometimes, when you _____, you don't have a care in the
         11. had ridden / are riding
world."

Read the following selection from Omni Magazine. *Choose the correct modal and verb combinations.*

Psychic Pooch

by Sherry Baker

After sustaining a head injury in a 1984 car crash, Victoria

Doroshenko suffered from daily, severe epileptic seizures.[1] She often

broke bones or injured her head when she fell during these episodes.

Then she _____ to a
       1. would frequently be confined / must frequently be confined

wheelchair. That's when the Washington state woman began searching

for a dog that _____ her belongings,
       2. can carry / could carry

pick up her crutches, or pull her wheelchair. The dog she found, a golden

retriever named Harley, turned out to be more help than Doroshenko

_____: Harley, it seems,
  3. could ever have imagined / could ever have imagine

_____ when she is about to have a seizure and
      4. can sense / can senses

warns her, sometimes up to 45 minutes before a seizure begins.

    Soon after taking Harley home, Doroshenko was startled when the dog

suddenly refused to obey commands and began running around her. "I sat down

and went into a grand mal,"[2] she says. "Ever since, Harley has been forewarning

me of seizures. He breaks my falls. If I'm alone, he'll go for help."

    How _____ a dog predict
       5. should / could

epileptic seizures? Reina Berner, executive director of the New York-based

Epilepsy Institute, suggests several possible explanations. Berner says

....
[1] **epileptic seizures** sudden attacks of epilepsy—a medical condition that can make a person become unconscious or unable to control his or her movements for short periods of time

[2] **grand mal** a serious epileptic seizure

....

Harley _____ detect mild behavioral

    6. may have been able to / may be able to

or physiological changes[3]—imperceptible[4] to humans—that a person

_____ before the onset of a seizure. "Or," says

    7. may exhibit / may exhibits

Berner, "it _____ that the animal somehow

    8. could have been / could be

picks up changes in the electromagnetic fields in the person's brain." Berner

_____ to isolate the cues Harley picks up on so

    9. would like / could like

that other dogs _____ as safety companions for

    10. can be trained / may have been trained

people with epilepsy.

"Before I got my dog," says Doroshenko, "I was afraid and housebound.

Harley gave me my life back."

....

[3] **physiological changes** changes in the body

[4] **imperceptible** impossible to see or notice

CHAPTER 3 Nouns and Determiners

Read the following selection from Alaska Airlines *magazine. Choose the correct determiner and noun form.*

Blue Wonder

by David George Gordon

Less than half a mile from shore, on _____ small boat

                                                     1. the / a

in central California's Monterey Bay, Brenda Peterson had an encounter with

nature she'll never forget. "Here we were, still within sight of land, when we came

across a huge superpod[1] of wild dolphins," the Seattle resident recalls. "We were

surrounded by maybe 1,500 of them, leaping clear of _____

                                                    2. the / a

water, again and again, with such speed that _____ bodies never

                                            3. their / its

seemed to touch down."

For Peterson and _____ 50 passengers on board, the

                                     4. other / the other

experience was incredible.

"There were splashes everywhere," she says. "We were surrounded by a

tsunami—a tidal wave[2] of dolphins."

"It's impossible to observe one of these active, highly intelligent

_____ without feeling a sense of respect," agrees Dr. Martin

    5. animals / animal

Haulena, staff veterinarian with the Marine Mammal Center, a nonprofit

organization in Sausalito, California. "_____ ocean dwellers

                              6. Little / Few

evoke[3] such emotional responses from _____ people."

                                    7. the / Ø

---

[1] **superpod** very large group

[2] **tidal wave** very large ocean wave

[3] **evoke** produce a strong feeling in someone

Blue Wonder by David George Gordon, a Seattle-based author. Reprinted by permission.
www.davidgeorgegordon.com

And with good reason. Unlike cold-blooded fish, dolphins and porpoises

possess what can best be described as *joie de vivre*—an undeniable zeal[4] for

_____ living. Whether leaping from the water to perform a
     8. the / Ø

cartwheel 10 feet in the air, or racing in front of a speeding pleasure boat to hitch

a ride on the vessel's bow wave,[5] these animals display an obvious delight and an

astounding sense of comfort and ease in their blue world.

     Beginning with Dr. John Lilly's work on _____ dolphin
                                  9. Ø / the

brain, some interesting and even controversial _____ has
                          10. research / researches

been done to assess[6] dolphin intelligence, social behavior, and communication.

_____ Scientists have discovered, for example, that when wild
     11. Ø / The

dolphins gather in large herds,[7] they form a definite hierarchy, with individuals

establishing places in the pecking order[8] with the aid of a "signature whistle"—a

highly pitched sound that all other _____ can hear and identify.
                 12. dolphin / dolphins

     Some _____ have theorized that these whistles,
        13. researcher / researchers

as well as clicks, clacking noises, and squeaks, may be a form of language

(nicknamed *dolphinspeak*), with which dolphins can share complex thoughts.

_____ people have tried to learn _____
   14. Much / Several   **15. this / these**

language, attempting to open the doors to future conversations with some of the

most intelligent cohabitants of our planet. . . .

....

[4] **zeal** great interest and eagerness

[5] **hitch a ride on the vessel's bow wave** be carried on a wave that is formed at the front of a boat

[6] **assess** measure

[7] **herd** group

[8] **pecking order** social order of a group of people or animals

Read the following selection from New University, the student newspaper from the University of California, Irvine. Choose the correct verb.

Latin American Film Explosion

by Frank Morales

Several Latin American films that are equivalent to Hollywood blockbusters[1]

_____ on campus in a series called the "Festival
1. will be shown / will be showed

of Latin American Cinema." In addition to a wide variety of foreign films, special

guest speakers and poetry readings will also be featured throughout the festival.

The series will present movies that _____
2. have collected / have been collected

from different parts of Latin America; countries such as Mexico, Chile, and

Argentina _____. According to Jacobo Sefami,
3. will be featured / will feature

associate professor of Spanish and chair of the Department of Spanish and

Portuguese, the film festival was created to provide scholarly perspectives[2] on how

different cultures are organized in different places throughout Latin America.

"The idea was to have a diverse type of festival where films

_____ from different countries and have different
4. present / are presented

story lines," Sefami said. "Love stories, political stories, and stories with a sense of

the diversity of Latin America are what _____ in
5. is being highlighted / is highlighting

this series."

According to Sefami, what _____ this
6. is made / makes

year's film festival different from last year's is the fact that more countries

_____ in the films.
7. are representing / are being represented

....

[1] **blockbusters** very successful movies

[2] **perspectives** ways of thinking that are influenced by one's personality, background, or work

....

New University Newspaper, April 10, 2000. Reprinted by permission.

"The idea was to expand on the previous festival, which

_____ on only Mexico," Sefami said. . . .
8. had focused / had been focus

The festival _____ as an alternative[3]
9. created / was created

method to educate students on campus.

The films are in the native language of where the film originates, but all of

the movies have English subtitles. Although Sefami said that sometimes people

_____ films with subtitles, he feels that once
10. do not attract to / are not attracted to

they try it out and continue to see movies with subtitles, they end up liking these

movies. . . .

Janine Curiel, a UCI student, commented on how important it is for the

university to be involved in providing a diverse education. . . . "Some students are

probably not even aware of the diversity that exists in their own communities. The

festival will be educational and fun at the same time."
....
[3] **alternative** different from what is usual or expected

CHAPTER 5 Word Forms and Commonly Confused Words

Read the following selection from The Daily Pilot, a local newspaper from southern California. Choose the correct word form or commonly confused word.

College in China a Choice

by Tom Ragen

For students who can't afford the cost of a higher education in the United

States, there's another _____ out there—way out there.
1. alternate / alternative

There's a four-year university in China that charges $12,750 a year.

Multiply that by four years and the total comes to $51,000. That equals

_____ the cost of one year's tuition at any Ivy League[1] or private
2. almost / most

university stateside.

It's just _____ example—and perhaps the wave of the
3. the other / another

future[2]—in which China has managed to undercut American prices, only this

time it's in the realm of education, said Rick Popovic, president of the New York-

based Study International, which handles registration for _____
4. interested / interesting

American students.

"And the price includes room, board, classes, textbooks, food and two

round-trip tickets back to the United States on a _____ basis,"
5. year / yearly

Popovic said.

So far, there are more than 100 students who have enrolled at the Nankai

University, near Beijing, Popovic said.

....

[1] **Ivy League** a group of U.S. colleges with high academic standards and prestige

[2] **the wave of the future** a belief or idea that many people feel will happen

Although there are an estimated 24,000 Chinese students who attend the university, there are 3,000 foreign students, 100 of whom have taken advantage so far of the new American program, Popovic said.

He said all the classes are taught in English, and that knowing Mandarin is not a _____, although it's _____ something

6. require / requirement   **7. certainly / certain**

students will pick up after a four-year term.

Although the majority of students are Chinese Americans, Popovic is urging everybody to weigh their options[3] before taking out the student loans and footing the bill.[4]

"Here's a chance to learn Mandarin and experience first-hand one of the fastest growing economies in the world, if not the _____

8. fast / fastest

growing," he said.

What's extra special about the program, Popovic said, is that credits are

_____ to the U.S.

9. transfer / transferable

"They can get a degree just like they would at a school here," he said, referring to American students. "It can be liberal arts, engineering, the sciences. This is a really _____ rated school that's been around since

10. highest / highly

1919."

....

[3] **weigh their options** consider all possible choices

[4] **footing the bill** paying for something that is usually expensive

CHAPTER 6 Verb Forms, Gerunds, and Infinitives

Read the following selection from Orange County Woman *magazine. Choose the correct verb form, gerund, or infinitive.*

Touched by an Angel
by Janine Robinson

Growing up poor in a Hispanic barrio,[1] Marie Moreno attended a

segregated,[2] all-Latino elementary school. But it wasn't until she moved into an

integrated school that she felt true discrimination.

Moreno, the third youngest of six children, was pelted with beer cans and

racist remarks when she walked to her new school in the third grade in the late

1940s. During classes she was reprimanded[3] for _____ Spanish.
                                      1. speaking / to speak

Even when her family eventually moved into a better, predominantly white

neighborhood, many children were prohibited from[4] _____ with
                                      2. play / playing

her. It was at this new school, which was forced _____ as a result
                                      3. integrating / to integrate

of federal legislation, that Moreno recognized a consequence of discrimination: the

education she had been denied.

"When I walked into these classes in the new, integrated school, I didn't

know what they were talking about. I realized I was so far behind. It made me

_____ we had not been getting the education in my old school
      4. realize / realized

that we were supposed to be getting," says Moreno, now 55.

At age eight she told her parents she wanted _____
                                      5. attend / to attend

the best private parochial school.[5] When her parents told her they could not

....

[1] **barrio** area in a city where many poor people live

[2] **segregated** separated from different groups or races

[3] **reprimanded** told someone that something they have done is very wrong

[4] **prohibited from** not allowed to

[5] **private parochial school** church school not part of free public school system

....

Orange County Woman Magazine, April 1999. Reprinted by permission.

_____ the college prep school, the young Moreno informed
6. afford / afforded

them she already had a job—at the local Catholic church.

With the help of her local priest, Moreno worked as the assistant

housekeeper on weekends, and over several years saved about $800. The nuns and

priests helped her _____ for the entrance exam. After she was
7. prepare / preparing

accepted in 1959, the nuns helped her sew her own school uniforms while she

worked nights and weekends.

After graduation Moreno attended college. Over the next decade she held

a series of jobs, where she built her marketing and public relations skills. Through

a friend, Moreno learned of an opening[6] with the Anaheim Angels[7] in 1993,

and was hired from among 700 applicants, mainly because of her involvement

with the Hispanic community. Moreno has been integral in numerous outreach

programs,[8] including the "Rookie Ball" program that allows low-income children

_____ on baseball teams for free, as well as other Angels-
8. to play / playing

sponsored free baseball clinics.

Moreno spends much of her time talking to students in the schools and

encourages them _____ their educations. "When I talk to kids,
9. to pursue / pursuing

I always let them _____ my background, where I was born and
10. know / to know

raised and that when they have a dream, the only one that can stop that dream is

themselves," she says.

....

6 opening job

7 Anaheim Angels professional baseball team in California

8 has been integral in numerous outreach programs has played an important role in programs that provide help and services

CHAPTER 7 Coordination and Parallel Structure

Read the following selection from the Indicator, *a magazine from California State University, Fullerton. Choose the forms for correct coordination and parallel structure.*

Service to Country: Four Military Veterans Return to Civilian Life and Join the Ranks of Mihaylo College
by Laurie McLaughlin

"The military is the ultimate crash course[1] in self-reliance. We're often pushed to the limits of endurance[2] in a _____, high-stress and
1. danger / dangerous
limited sleep environment, so you have to rely on yourself," says Army Spc. Gary Miller II, who served from 2002 to 2006. "Military service taught me self-discipline because we had to do what was necessary no matter what the conditions were," he said. "We didn't have everything we needed, _____ we had to
2. so / or
make use of what was available to accomplish tasks. And we did."

Miller is one of several military veterans who has returned to the civilian ranks,[3] opening a new chapter in his career and _____ the skills
3. applying / to apply
he's learned to earning a business degree.

"Like many Americans, I was called to protect my country after September 11," says Army Sgt. Jason Fagan, who served as an Army intelligence analyst[4] and linguist for five years and is now pursuing a bachelor's in finance. "Joining was especially meaningful because both my father _____ grandfather
4. and / but
served, _____ my family also stressed the importance of an
5. so / but
education. . . ."

....

[1] **crash course** a course in which you learn to do a lot in a short period of time

[2] **endurance** ability to do something difficult over a long period of time

[3] **civilian ranks** people who are not part of the military

[4] **intelligence analyst** a job that requires analysis of information to help make decisions about public safety and security

....

"The Army values—loyalty, duty, _____,

6. respect, honor / respectful, honorable

and integrity—guide me in my everyday life," says student and Army Sgt. Adan

Flores, who served in South Korea.

"The leadership skills that I learned in the service have helped me become

a leader in the classroom _____ will help me throughout my

7. or / and

career," adds Fagan.

The mix of _____ and business is considered a benefit

8. disciplinary / discipline

among military veterans, _____ each soldier navigates the

9. but / so

transition from military to civilian life differently. "For me, the adjustment wasn't

difficult. College is easier than the military," says economics student Marine Cpl.

Clay Narey, who was on two combat tours in Iraq as a rifleman. Narey is also vice

president of the Cal State Fullerton Student Veterans Association, which provides

_____ , mentoring,[5] _____, and a sense of

10. resourceful / resources   11. guidance / guide

community for military veterans transitioning to a campus routine. . . .

The veterans have taken advantage of the synergies[6] provided by

_____ the military and academia: "The goal of the Army is to

12. both / neither

develop a soldier of character who can make _____

13. logical and ethic / logical and ethical

decisions that will bring honor to his country and fellow soldiers," he says. . . .

"The goals [of the military and a business education] are similar

_____ the tactics[7] are different."

14. but / so

....

[5] **mentoring** a system in which people with a lot of experience or knowledge help others without this experience or knowledge

[6] **synergies** additional effectiveness when people or groups work together

[7] **tactics** methods used to achieve something

CHAPTER 8 Adjective Clauses

Read the following selection from OC Family Magazine. Choose the correct form and use of adjective clauses.

Get on the Piano

by Christopher Trela

Taking piano lessons and solving math puzzles _____

1. that / where

are on a computer significantly improve specific math skills of elementary

schoolchildren, according to a new study.

The results, which _____ in the

2. were published / they were published

March issue of the journal *Neurological Research,* are the latest in a series

_____ links musical training to the development of higher brain

3. who / that

functions.

Researchers _____ worked with 135 second-grade

4. which / who

students at the 95th Street School in Los Angeles first conducted a pilot study[1] with

102 students. Children _____ were given four months of piano

5. which / that

training as well as time playing with newly designed computer software scored 27

percent higher on math and fraction tests than other children.

Piano instruction is thought to enhance the brain's "hard wiring"[2] for

spatial-temporal reasoning, or the ability to visualize and transform objects in

space and time, says physics professor Gordon Shaw _____ who

6. , / Ø

led the study.

....

[1] pilot study test that is done to see if an idea or product will be successful

[2] hard wiring permanent structure

....

At the same time, the computer game allows children to solve geometric

and math puzzles that _____ their ability to manipulate shapes

7. boosts / boost

in their mind.

The findings are significant because a grasp of proportional math

and fractions is a prerequisite[3] to math at higher levels, and children who

_____ master these areas of math cannot understand more

8. do not / does not

advanced math that _____ critical[4] to high-tech fields.

9. it is / is

Students _____ used the software and played the piano

10. whom / who

also demonstrated a heightened ability to think ahead, Shaw says. "They were able

to leap ahead several steps on problems in their heads."

Researchers plan to expand the study to six schools this fall to demonstrate

its effectiveness in a variety of settings.

....

[3] **prerequisite** requirement

[4] **critical** very important

Read the following selection from New University, *the student newspaper from the University of California, Irvine. Choose the correct form and use of adverb clauses and conditionals.*

Feng Shui Rearranges Your Qi

by Melinda Sheckells

The rebirth of Feng Shui, the ancient Chinese science of architectural design, became very popular in the interior design world in the 1990s and has since become a necessity in modern architecture.

Donna Huhem, a practitioner of non-traditional Feng Shui, fell in love with the ancient science _____ she attended a weekend seminar.

                        1. after / unless

"_____ I took the first class, it made sense to me. I

              2. When / Where

understood things about my own house," Huhem said. . . .

The *New University* invited Huhem into its offices to evaluate the work space and to answer the question "Does the *New U.* have good qi?"[1]

Huhem used the bagua[2] to evaluate the office of Editor-in-Chief Shaya Mohajer. . . .

_____ Huhem evaluates a space, she says that she first

        3. Because / When

discusses with the client what they feel is going on in their lives as well as what they would like to change about their surroundings.

"Number 1, Feng Shui is about change," Huhem said. "The most common complaint from clients is that something just doesn't feel right about the space or the room."

....

[1] **qi** energy in a room (pronounced "chee")

[2] **bagua** a grid that sections off a space into nine areas in order to evaluate the space

....

New University Newspaper, January 15, 2001. Reprinted with Permission.

Huhem asked Mohajer if she felt there _____ challenges
                                        4. were / are
to her authority within the office. Mohajer pinpointed that she wanted her office

space to reflect a stronger position of leadership.

After Huhem and Mohajer verbally consulted, Huhem evaluated Mohajer's

office using the bagua, which divides the room into nine imaginary sectors: power,

future, relationships, descendents, compassion, self, wisdom, community, and

health.

Huhem suggested that Mohajer could strengthen her relationship with the

staff if she _____ her desk out of direct alignment[3] with the door
              5. moved / moves
and positioned her chair so there is a wall to her back.

"There is nothing to block the negative energy if the desk

_____ in direct alignment with the door," Huhem said, noting
    6. were / is
that during home consultations she also advises clients to move the bed out of

direct alignment with an entranceway.

"If your back is exposed, people _____ up on you,"
                                   7. could sneak / can sneak
Huhem said.

Huhem advised that to maintain a positive flow of qi, Mohajer should get

rid of 25 things in her office.

"If you _____ use it, get it out," Huhem said.
          8. don't / didn't
According to Huhem, clutter[4] is the number one qi-blocker.

"Feng Shui means wind/water and clutter is stagnant; it doesn't allow water

to flow," Huhem said.

....
[3] **alignment** arrangement in a line

[4] **clutter** many things left in a messy way

The water principle of Feng Shui shows itself in the elements that we can see, such as interiors and room decorations. However, the wind principle is more philosophical.

"_____ We can't see the wind, but we can see its effects.

        9. Although / Ø

We want qi to flow like a gentle breeze," Huhem said. . . .

On a final note, Huhem advised that the *New U.* staff area should also be rearranged to reflect the positive changes that will be made to Mohajer's office space. The *New U.* editorial staff currently uses desks that are separated by high partitions.

Huhem feels that _____ these work spaces don't allow

        10. because / even though

colleagues to face one another, they don't produce positive energy.

"Cubicles this high tend to isolate people from one another," Huhem said. "It's hard to have your vision go beyond the box. It is a bad space for someone who wants to move forward. There is also no support from the back."

Huhem promised that once Mohajer and the *New U.* staff implement these special changes, the editorial offices will be flowing with positive qi.

CHAPTER 11 Prepositions

Read the following selection from the Coast Report, the student newspaper from Orange Coast College. Choose the correct prepositions. Use a dictionary and Appendix 5 to look up new preposition combinations that you are not familiar with.

Spring: Nature's Way of Saying 'Let's Party'
by Hannah Fry

Take a look outside. The sky is getting bluer, the days longer, and the

temperatures warmer.

As students respond _____ the rising thermometer, they
                  1. for / to

begin stripping _____ their winter garb[1] in exchange for sandals,
           2. on / off

shorts, and, well, basically, more skin-revealing clothes.

Although it has yet to be proven _____ the experts, many
              3. by / on

scientists believe that _____ springtime the warm weather and
       4. on / in

shedding of clothes brings out more pheromones—chemicals of attraction.

Whatever it is, it's springtime—time for love and romance. While there may

not be a clinical definition _____ the symptoms that go with it,
          5. for / by

many people just attribute their fatigue and apathy[2] or excitement and energy to

one thing: spring fever.

Spring fever can be characterized by low energy, fatigue, and apathy in

the early spring season. As spring continues and the day length increases, people

become overwhelmed _____ a sense _____
        6. with / in   **7. for / of**

excitement and energy.

....

[1] garb a particular style of clothing

[2] apathy lack of interest

Charlene Melrose, a psychology professor at Orange Coast College, said

although spring fever isn't an actual condition, there are changes in the body that

might affect a person's mood.

Melrose said these changes, scientifically speaking, are a result

_____ melatonin levels decreasing _____
       8. by / of   **9. during / on**

periods of increased sunlight. Melatonin is a hormone that affects sleep cycles and

mood changes.

"More melatonin is released _____ winter months, when
                                        10. in / at

there are longer nights and longer periods of darkness. Many people report more

energy _____ the spring months, when there are shorter nights
           11. to / during

and there is a decrease in melatonin production," Melrose said.

Melrose said although spring fever is a vague[3] term, researchers

have addressed mood and behavior changes during the spring season. The

Virginia Institute for Psychiatric and Behavioral Genetics studied 500 people

_____ the U.S. and Canada and documented that better moods
        12. at / in

followed spending more time outside _____ spring days, full
                                      13. on / in

_____ bright sunshine.
        14. by / of

"People's focus at times changes with the seasons," Melrose said.

"During times of more light and nicer weather, people start to think ahead

_____ summer."
        15. for / toward

....

[3] **vague** unclear or not specific

Britnee Pinkerton, an 18-year-old undecided major, said that during

spring break she stayed _____ home playing video games
16. at / in

_____ the Internet.
17. on / by

"The first day back was tiring," Pinkerton said. "When spring hits, it's

always much more difficult to be _____ school."
18. at / on

Melrose said she read an article recently that says that human conception

spikes _____ mid-June, right before summer begins. There is
19. in / between

a 20 percent higher rate of conception[4] toward the end _____
20. for / of

spring.

"Even poets seem to point to spring as a time to enjoy love and romance,"

Melrose said.

....
[4] **conception** process by which a person becomes pregnant

APPENDIX 2: IRREGULAR VERBS

Base Form	Simple Past	Past Participle	Base Form	Simple Past	Past Participle
awake	awoke	awoken	fight	fought	fought
be	was, were	been	find	found	found
beat	beat	beaten/beat	fit	fit	fit
become	became	become	flee	fled	fled
begin	began	begun	fly	flew	flown
bend	bent	bent	forbid	forbade	forbidden
bet	bet	bet	forecast	forecast	forecast
bind	bound	bound	forget	forgot	forgotten
bite	bit	bitten	forgive	forgave	forgiven
bleed	bled	bled	freeze	froze	frozen
blow	blew	blown	get	got	gotten/got
break	broke	broken	give	gave	given
bring	brought	brought	go	went	gone
broadcast	broadcast	broadcast	grind	ground	ground
build	built	built	grow	grew	grown
burn	burned	burned	hang	hung	hung
buy	bought	bought	have	had	had
catch	caught	caught	hear	heard	heard
choose	chose	chosen	hide	hid	hidden
cling	clung	clung	hit	hit	hit
come	came	come	hold	held	held
cost	cost	cost	hurt	hurt	hurt
creep	crept	crept	keep	kept	kept
cut	cut	cut	know	knew	known
deal	dealt	dealt	lay	laid	laid
dig	dug	dug	lead	led	led
dive	dove/dived	dived	leave	left	left
do	did	done	lend	lent	lent
draw	drew	drawn	let	let	let
dream	dreamed/dreamt	dreamed/dreamt	lie	lay	lain
drink	drank	drunk	light	lit/lighted	lit/lighted
drive	drove	driven	lose	lost	lost
eat	ate	eaten	make	made	made
fall	fell	fallen	mean	meant	meant
feed	fed	fed	meet	met	met
feel	felt	felt	mislead	misled	misled

Base Form	Simple Past	Past Participle	Base Form	Simple Past	Past Participle
mistake	mistook	mistaken	split	split	split
misunderstand	misunderstood	misunderstood	spread	spread	spread
overcome	overcame	overcome	spring	sprang	sprung
pay	paid	paid	stand	stood	stood
prove	proved	proven/proved	steal	stole	stolen
put	put	put	stick	stuck	stuck
quit	quit	quit	sting	stung	stung
read	read	read	stink	stank/stunk	stunk
rid	rid	rid	strike	struck	struck/stricken
ride	rode	ridden	string	strung	strung
ring	rang	rung	strive	strove/strived	striven
rise	rose	risen	swear	swore	sworn
run	ran	run	sweep	swept	swept
say	said	said	swim	swam	swum
see	saw	seen	swing	swung	swung
seek	sought	sought	take	took	taken
sell	sold	sold	teach	taught	taught
send	sent	sent	tear	tore	torn
set	set	set	tell	told	told
sew	sewed	sewn/sewed	think	thought	thought
shake	shook	shaken	throw	threw	thrown
shed	shed	shed	understand	understood	understood
shine	shone/shined	shone/shined	undertake	undertook	undertaken
shoot	shot	shot	undo	undid	undone
show	showed	shown	uphold	upheld	upheld
shrink	shrank/shrunk	shrunk/shrunken	upset	upset	upset
shut	shut	shut	wake	woke	woken/waked
sing	sang	sung	wear	wore	worn
sit	sat	sat	weave	wove	woven
sleep	slept	slept	weep	wept	wept
slide	slid	slid	wet	wet	wet
speak	spoke	spoken	win	won	won
speed	sped/speeded	sped/speeded	wind	wound	wound
spend	spent	spent	withdraw	withdrew	withdrawn
spin	spun	spun	write	wrote	written
spit	spit/spat	spat			

APPENDIX 3: SUBJECT-VERB AGREEMENT

Subject-verb agreement means that a verb must agree with its subject. It must agree in person and in number. Here are some examples of subject-verb agreement listed by verb tense.

SIMPLE PRESENT			
SINGULAR		**PLURAL**	
I	work.	We	work.
You	work.	You	work.
He/She/It	works.	They	work.

SIMPLE PAST			
SINGULAR		**PLURAL**	
I	worked.	We	worked.
You	worked.	You	worked.
He/She/It	worked.	They	worked.

PRESENT PROGRESSIVE			
SINGULAR		**PLURAL**	
I	am working.	We	are working.
You	are working.	You	are working.
He/She/It	is working.	They	are working.

PAST PROGRESSIVE			
SINGULAR		**PLURAL**	
I	was working.	We	were working.
You	were working.	You	were working.
He/She/It	was working.	They	were working.

PRESENT PERFECT			
SINGULAR		**PLURAL**	
I	have worked.	We	have worked.
You	have worked.	You	have worked.
He/She/It	has worked.	They	have worked.

PAST PERFECT			
SINGULAR		**PLURAL**	
I	had worked before.	We	had worked before.
You	had worked before.	You	had worked before.
He/She/It	had worked before.	They	had worked before.

Subject-Verb Agreement Rules

1. There can be only one –*s* ending. It is either on the subject or on the verb.

   *An advertisement help***s** *sell products to the public.* / *Advertisement***s** *help sell products to the public.*

2. In the simple present, add an –*s* ending to most verbs that follow third-person singular subjects.

   Billy's uncle *live***s** *near the fire station.*

   In many cultures, <u>one</u> *leave***s** *home for the first time after marriage.*

3. A subject and verb must agree even when separated by a clause or phrase.

   The company *that hired those engineers* **produces** *computer chips.*

4. The correlative conjunctions *both . . . and, either . . . or,* and *neither . . . nor* follow subject-verb agreement rules.

   - Use the plural verb with *both . . . and*.

     Both *buying real estate* **and** *investing in the stock market* <u>are</u> *good long-term investment strategies.*

   - The closest noun and verb must agree with *either . . . or* and *neither . . . nor.*

     Either *the hospital* **or** <u>*pharmacies supply*</u> *the medicine she needs.* / **Either** *pharmacies* **or** *the* <u>*hospital supplies*</u> *the medicine she needs.*

     Neither *lotion* **nor** *special* <u>*creams erase*</u> *the signs of aging.* / **Neither** *special creams* **nor** <u>*lotion erases*</u> *the signs of aging.*

APPENDIX 4: PUNCTUATION

Use this appendix of rules as a reference for correct punctuation, capitalization, and use of underlining, italics, or quotation marks with titles in your writing.

Periods, Question Marks, and Exclamation Points

1. Use a period to end a sentence.
   There is a test next Monday.
2. Use a question mark to end a direct question.
   Do we have to study?
3. Use an exclamation point to end a sentence that expresses surprise, excitement, or anger.
   The test is tomorrow!

Comma

1. Use a comma to separate words, phrases, or clauses in a series.
   We brought sandwiches, juice, and cookies to the party.
   The cross country team ran through the park, up the hill, and by the library.
   Their oldest child plays the piano, the middle child sings, and the youngest acts in plays.
2. Use a comma to separate independent clauses joined by a coordinating conjunction.
   It is a beautiful day for swimming, but the pool is closed.
3. Use a comma after introducing an adverbial phrase or clause.
   On the last day of school, students and teachers usually celebrate.
   Although the price of gasoline is going up, people are still traveling by car.
4. Use a comma with nonrestrictive adjective clauses.
   Valentine's Day, which is celebrated on February 14, is a very busy day for florists.

Semicolon

1. Use a semicolon to link closely related independent clauses.
   The election is tomorrow; the polls open at 7:00 A.M.
2. Use a semicolon or period before the transitions *however, nevertheless, nonetheless, therefore, moreover, furthermore, otherwise,* and *thus.* Notice that commas are used after transitions.
   Julia will graduate in a few months; therefore, she has started to look for a job in her field.
   Julia will graduate in a few months. Therefore, she has started to look for a job in her field.

Colon

Use a colon to introduce a series of examples after an independent clause.
The salad had three ingredients: tomatoes, cucumbers, and lettuce.

Capitalization

1. **Capitalize proper nouns.**

Names of people and their titles	John Smith, Dr. Joan Chavez, Aunt Dorothy, Professor Yi
Names of places and things	the Eiffel Tower, the University of New Mexico, the Golden Gate Bridge
Names of countries	Canada, the Philippines, Indonesia, Nepal
Names of languages	French, Spanish, Hebrew, English
Names of nationalities	German, American, Indian, Costa Rican
Names of religions	Buddhism, Catholicism, Judaism, Islam
Names of academic courses	Biology 101, Humanities 200A, World Religions
Directional names	the East Coast, the Deep South, the North Pole, Southern Florida

2. **Capitalize proper adjectives.**

Names of nationalities	French crepes, Mexican restaurant, Chinese artifact
Names of religions	Jewish nation, Christian people, Buddhist monk
Names of brands	Apple computer, Nike running shoes, Bayer aspirin

3. **Do not capitalize:**

Names of seasons	summer, winter, spring, fall/autumn
Articles, prepositions	the United States, the Department of Chemistry
After a semicolon	My brother is a baseball fanatic; he goes to every home game.

Underline or Italicize

Titles of books	The Great Gatsby, *Grammar for Writing*
Titles of magazines	*Sports Illustrated*, Time
Titles of newspapers	The New York Times, *The Wall Street Journal*
Titles of movies and plays	*E.T.*, African Queen, *A Chorus Line*, Cats

Quotation Marks

Titles of short stories	"The Legacy," "The Twenty-Seventh Man"
Titles of articles in a newspaper or magazine	"Economic Outlook Looks Bright," "Get on the Piano"
Titles of poems	"Beautiful Old Age," "Birches"

APPENDIX 5: PREPOSITIONS

This appendix includes a list of frequently used adjective-preposition combinations and a list of common verb-preposition combinations. Use these lists as a reference while writing.

Adjective + Preposition Combinations

Check an ESL or learner's dictionary under the adjective for additional adjective + preposition combinations.

A
accustomed to
afraid of
amazed at/by
angry at
anxious about
ashamed of
aware of
awful at

B
bad at
bored with/by

C
capable of
concerned about
content with
curious about

D
dependent on
different from

E
eager for
envious of
excited about

F
familiar with
fond of
friendly to
full of
famous for

G
glad about
good at
guilty of

H
happy about
homesick for

I
inferior to
interested in

J
jealous of

K
known for

L
limited to
lucky at

M
mad at/about

N
nervous about

O
opposed to

P
pleased about
proud of

R
ready for
responsible for

S
sad about
safe from
satisfied with
sick of
similar to
slow at
sorry for/about
suitable for
superior to
surprised about/
   at/by

T
tired of
terrible at

U
upset with

W
worried about

Verb + Preposition Combinations

Check an ESL dictionary under the verb for additional verb + preposition combinations.

A
accuse someone of something
adapt to
admit to
advise against
agree with someone about something
apologize for
apply to/for
approve of
argue with someone about something
arrive at

B
believe in
belong to
blame someone for something

C
care about/for
choose between
combine something with
come from
compare something to/with something
complain about something
complain to someone
concentrate on
consist of
contribute to
cooperate with
count on

D

deal with

decide on

depend on

disapprove of

dream about/of

E

escape from

excel at

excuse someone for

F

feel like

fight for

forget about

forgive someone for

G

glance at

gossip about

graduate from

H

happen to

hear about/of something

hear from someone

hide from

hope for

I

insist on

intend to

interfere with

introduce someone to

invite someone to something

K

know about

L

listen to

look at

look for

look forward to

learn from

M

matter to

O

object to

P

participate in

pay for

plan on

prepare for

prevent someone or something from

profit from

protect someone or something from

prohibit someone from

R

read about

recover from

rely on

rescue from

respond to

S

search for

speak to/with someone about something

stare at

subscribe to

substitute for

succeed in/at

T

take advantage of

take care of

talk to/with someone about something

thank someone for something

think about/of

V

vote for

W

wait for

worry about

APPENDIX 6: PHRASAL VERBS

A phrasal verb is a combination of a verb and one or two particles. Particles and prepositions look the same, but particles change the meaning of the verb. Phrasal verbs are commonly used in informal speech; there is usually a more formal verb that has the same meaning. For example, *select* is considered more formal than *pick out*. The following is a list of some commonly used phrasal verbs. Use this list as a reference while writing.

A

ask out	ask someone for a date

B

break up	end a relationship
bring up	rise children / introduce a topic

C

call back	return a phone call
call off	cancel
call on	visit someone / ask a student to speak in a class
call up	call on the telephone
catch on	understand / become popular
catch up with	reach the same level
check in	register at a hotel
check into	investigate
check out	borrow a book from the library / investigate
check out of	leave a hotel
check up on	make sure something is done correctly by someone
cheer up	make someone feel better
clean up	make clean
come across	meet someone without prior arrangement / find something accidentally
come out	become known
cross out	draw a line through
cut out	stop an irritating activity

D

do over	repeat
drop by	visit without an invitation
drop off	take someone or something someplace
drop out of	to stop going to school or doing an activity

F

figure out	understand (after thinking about)
fill out	complete a form or questionnaire
fill up	fill completely
find out	discover information

G

get along with	be friendly with someone
get back from	return
get in	enter a car / arrive in a place
get off	leave an airplane, bicycle, bus, subway, train
get on	enter an airplane, bicycle, bus, subway, train

get out of	leave a car / avoid work or an unpleasant activity
get over	become well after a sickness
get through	finish
get up	rise from a bed or chair
give back	return something to its owner
give in	agree after disagreement
give up	stop trying
go out	leave home for entertainment
go over	review
grow up	become an adult

H

hand in	give an assignment to a teacher or supervisor
hand out	distribute
hang out	spend time in a particular way / spend time with particular people
hang up	finish a telephone call / put clothes on a hanger
have on	wear clothing
help out	assist

K

keep on	continue
keep out of	not enter / not allow someone to enter
keep up with	go as fast as
kick out	force someone to leave

L

leave out	do not include
look after	take care of
look into	investigate
look over	review carefully
look up	try to find in a book or on the Internet

M

make up	invent / complete late work

N

name after / for	give a baby someone else's name

P

pass away	die
pass out	faint / distribute
pick out	select
pick up	go to get someone in a car / take something into one's hand
point out	call attention to
put away	put something in its proper place
put back	return something to its original place
put off	postpone
put on	put clothes on
put out	extinguish a cigarette or fire
put up with	tolerate

Q

quiet down	become quiet

R

run into / across	meet without prior arrangement
run out of	finish the supply of something

S

show off	behave boastfully
show up	appear
shut off	stop a machine, light, faucet
shut up	stop talking
speak up	talk louder / give an opinion
stay up	remain awake

T

take after	resemble
take off	remove clothing / leave on a trip
take out	remove something / take someone on a date
take over	take control
take up	begin a new activity
tear down	demolish
tear up	rip into small pieces
think over	consider carefully
throw away / out	get rid of
throw up	vomit
try on	put clothing on to see if it fits
try out	audition / test
turn down	decrease volume / reject an offer
turn in	go to bed / submit an assignment
turn off	stop a machine, light, faucet
turn on	start a machine, put on a light or faucet
turn out	extinguish a light
turn up	increase (volume)

U

use up	use completely

W

wake up	stop sleeping
watch out	be careful
wear out	become weak or useless

APPENDIX 7: PROBLEM WORDS AND PHRASES

This list includes some commonly misused words and phrases. As you come across other words and phrases that are problems for you, add them to this list. For practice with some of these problem words and phrases, refer to Chapter 5, Word Forms and Commonly Confused Words, in this book and to *Grammar for Writing 1* Chapter 11, Commonly Confused Words.

- ***Advice* (noncount noun) / *advise* (verb)**
*She gave me some good **advice**.*
*I **advised** him not to drop the class.*

- ***Affect* (verb) / *effect* (count noun)**
*Jim's worries **affected** his work.*
*Jim's worries had a negative **effect** on his work.*

- ***Agree on + something / agree with + someone***
*We **agreed on** all the answers.*
*She **agrees with** her father.*

- ***All of a sudden***
***All of a sudden** the electricity went out.*
NOT
All of the sudden . . .

- ***As a result***
*I passed the test. **As a result,** I can get my license.*
NOT
As the result . . .

- ***Because* (+ clause) / *because of* (+ noun)**
***Because** she had an appointment, she couldn't leave early.*
***Because** of the appointment, she couldn't leave early.*

- ***Belief* (count noun) / *believe* (verb)**
*They have strong **beliefs**.*
*They **believe** in truth and justice.*

- ***Beside* (next to) / *besides* (in addition to)**
*He sat **beside** me at the ceremony.*
***Besides** working together, we also take a class in the evening.*

- ***Had better***
*You **had better** see a doctor.*
*You**'d better** see a doctor.*
NOT
You better . . .

- ***Care about* (to be interested in) / *care for* (to take care of)**
*Some students don't **care about** their grades.*
*I have to **care for** my grandmother.*
NOT
I have to care about her.

- ***Concern* / *to be concerned about***
*Environmental problems **concern** me.*
*I **am concerned about** environmental problems.*

- ***Day after day***
*We study **day after day** to improve our knowledge.*
NOT
We study days after days . . .

- ***Despite***
***Despite** her effort, she couldn't pass the exam.*
NOT
Despite of her effort . . .

- ***Different from***
*I am **different from** my friends.*
NOT
I am different than . . .

- ***Each* / *every* + singular noun**
*At the party, **each** child gets a toy.*
***Every** mother loves her children.*

- ***Emphasize* / *to put emphasis on***
*The instructor **emphasized** the importance of grammar.*
*She **put** a lot of **emphasis on** verbs.*
NOT
The instructor emphasized on grammar.

- ***Even* (adverb / intensifier)**
*He doesn't **even** know his father.*
NOT
He even doesn't know . . .

- ***Exist***
*Those problems **exist** everywhere.*
NOT
Problems are exist . . .

- **Face / to be faced with**

We **face** new issues every day.

We **are faced with** new issues every day.

- **Hope**

I **hoped** you would come.

I **hope** you can come. I **hope** you will come.

NOT

I hope you would come.

- **In other words**

It's broken. **In other words,** it doesn't work.

NOT

In another word . . .

- **In spite of**

In spite of her diet, she couldn't lose weight.

NOT

In spite her diet . . .

- **In the first place**

In the first place, you should obey the law.

NOT

In a first place . . .

- **It doesn't matter if**

It doesn't matter if they are late.

NOT

It doesn't matter they are late.

- **Know / meet**

I **met** him in high school.

I **have known** him since then.

Note: Use *meet* not *know* when talking about first getting to know someone.

- **Most / most of the**

Most children obey their parents.

Most of the children obey their parents.

NOT

Most of children obey their parents.

- **Nowdays**

Nowadays, most people have computers.

NOT

Now a days . . .

- **On campus**

We want to live on **campus.**

NOT

We want to live in campus.

- **One of the** (+ plural noun)

One of the men has a new car.

NOT

One of the man . . .

- **People**

The **people** are living in poverty.

NOT

The people is . . .

- **Would rather**

He **would rather** be in China.

He**'d rather** be in China.

NOT

He rather be . . .

- **Succeed** (verb) / **success** (noun) / **successful** (adjective)

We **succeed** because we value **success** and we want to be **successful.**

- **Than** (conjunction with comparatives) / **then** (adverb, meaning *at that time*)

I am taller now **than** I was **then.**

- **the United States**

We live in **the United States** now.

NOT

We live in United States now.

- **Wish** (for things that are not real/true)— **hope** (for things that are possible)

She **wishes** she had a pet.

She **hopes** she gets a pet soon.

NOT

She wishes she has a pet.

- **Year-old / years old**

He is a **ten-year-old** boy.

He is **ten years old.**

NOT

He is a ten years old boy

APPENDIX 8: CORRECTION SYMBOLS

Your teacher may use symbols to indicate specific error types in your writing. The charts below include symbols, explanations, and sample sentences for some of these errors. You can use these symbols to help make the necessary corrections while editing your own work. Chart 1 refers to grammar items that are presented in *Grammar for Writing 2*. For further explanation and practice, refer to the appropriate chapters or appendices. Chart 2 presents other common correction symbols.

CHART 1

SYMBOL	MEANING	SAMPLE SENTENCE	*GRAMMAR FOR WRITING 2*
cs	comma splice (using a comma to connect two sentences)	cs It was a beautiful day, there wasn't a cloud in the sky.	Chapter 7
det	determiner error	det It is a most interesting book that I have read.	Chapter 3
frag	fragment (a partial sentence punctuated as a complete sentence)	frag When we practice. The team must work together.	Chapters 9, 10
id	problem with idioms or set expressions	id We always agree to our teachers.	Chapter 11 Appendices 5, 7
num	noun error (number)	num We have enough homeworks to last a week.	Chapter 3
p	punctuation error	p I remember, graduation as the most memorable event.	Chapters 7, 8, 9, 10 Appendix 4
ro	run on (two or more sentences without punctuation between them)	ro The lecture was very interesting it went by so fast.	Chapter 7
s-v	subject-verb error	s-v She never go to the library to study.	Chapters 1, 8 Appendix 3
t	verb tense error	t We haven't completed the project yesterday.	Chapter 1
vb	verb form error	vb They haven't went to the gym in weeks.	Chapters 1, 2, 4, 6, 10 Appendix 2
wf	word form error	wf Her father is the most success software engineer in the firm.	Chapters 5, 7
//	faulty parallelism	// We hoped for relaxation, peace and to have good weather.	Chapter 7

CHART 2

SYMBOL	MEANING	SAMPLE SENTENCE
prn	pronoun error	prn My friend and <u>me</u> went to the movies.
ref	unclear pronoun reference	ref We enjoyed the book and the movie, but <u>it</u> was more violent.
sp	spelling error	sp My apartment is <u>noisey</u> and expensive.
ww	wrong word	ww He is the best offensive player <u>in</u> the team.
^	insert missing word	in They are interested ^ going with us to the concert.
℘	delete	His writing is clear, and concise, and interesting to read.
¶	paragraph	This is the main theme. ¶ A secondary theme explains . . .
#	add a space	# My friends went to the club eventhough it's very expensive.
⟲	move here	The essay was interesting that we stayed up all night writing.
⌐	transpose	We hardly could remember the way to your house.

APPENDIX 9: EDITING LOG

Use this editing log or create a similar one of your own to keep track of the grammar errors that you make in your writing. By logging and correcting your errors, you will begin to see which errors you make the most frequently. Once you recognize the grammar topics that are the most problematic for you, editing becomes easier.

ERROR	SYMBOL	ORIGINAL SENTENCE	REVISED SENTENCE
Parallel Structure	//	My father's strength, wisdom, and determine have influenced my life.	My father's strength, wisdom, and determination have influenced my life.

APPENDIX 10: GRAMMAR BOOK REFERENCES

GRAMMAR FOR WRITING 2	FUNDAMENTALS OF ENGLISH GRAMMAR, FOURTH EDITION	UNDERSTANDING AND USING ENGLISH GRAMMAR, FOURTH EDITION	FOCUS ON GRAMMAR 4, FOURTH EDITION
Chapter 1 Tenses and Time Shifts	Chapter 1 Present Time:1–1, 1–2, 1–4 Chapter 2 Past Time: 2–1, 2–3, 2–4, 2–6, 2–8 Chapter 3 Future Time: 3–1, 3–2, 3–3, 3–4, 3–7, 3–8 Chapter 4 Present Perfect and Past Perfect: 4–1, 4–2, 4–4, 4–5, 4–6, 4–7, 4–8 Chapter 6: Nouns and Pronouns: 6–7	Chapter 1 Overview of the Verb Tenses: 1–1, 1–2, 1–3, 1–4, 1–5 Chapter 2 Present and Past; Simple and Progressive: 2–1, 2–2, 2–5, 2–7, 2–8 Chapter 3 Perfect and Perfect Progressive Tenses: 3–1, 3–3, 3–4, 3–5, 3–7 Chapter 4 Future Time: 4–1, 4–2, 4–4, 4–5, 4–6 Chapter 5 Review of Verb Tenses Chapter 6 Subject-Verb Agreement: 6–2	Part I Present and Past: Review and Expansion Part II Future: Review and Expansion
Chapter 2 Modals	Chapter 3 Future Time: 3–4 Chapter 7 Modal Auxiliaries: 7–1, 7–2, 7–3, 7–4, 7–5, 7–6, 7–7, 7–8, 7–9, 7–10, 7–11 Chapter 10 The Passive: 10–5	Chapter 9 Modals, Part 1: 9–1, 9–2, 9–3, 9–5, 9–6, 9–7, 9–8, 9–9, 9–12 Chapter 10 Modals, Part 2: 10–1, 10–2, 10–3, 10–4, 10–6, 10–7, 10–10	Part VII Modals: Review and Expansion Part 19 The Passive with Modals and Similar Expressions
Chapter 3 Nouns and Determiners	Chapter 6 Nouns and Pronouns: 6–1 Chapter 11 Count/Noncount Nouns and Articles: 11–1, 11–2, 11–4, 11–5, 11–6, 11–7, 11–8, 11–9	Chapter 7 Nouns: 7–1, 7–4, 7–5, 7–6, 7–7, 7–8, 7–9, 7–10, 7–11	–
Chapter 4 The Passive Voice	Chapter 10 The Passive Voice: 10–1, 10–2, 10–3, 10–5, 10–7	Chapter 11 The Passive Chapter 15: 15–4, 15–8	Part VIII The Passive
Chapter 5 Word Forms and Commonly Confused Words	Chapter 9 Comparisons: 9–2, 9–3, 9–7, 9–10	none	–
Chapter 6 Verb Forms, Gerunds, and Infinitives	Chapter 1 Present Time: 1–2 Chapter 2 Past Time: 2–1, 2–6 Chapter 4 Present Perfect and Past Perfect: 4–1 Chapter 7 Modal Auxiliaries: 7–1 Chapter 13 Gerunds and Infinitives: 13–1, 13–3, 13–4, 13–5,	Chapter 1: 1–5 Chapter 9: 9–1 Chapter 14 Chapter 15	Part I Present and Past: Review and Expansion Part II Future: Review and Expansion Unit 15 Modals and Similar Expressions: Review Part IV Gerunds and Infinitives Unit 20 The Passive Causative
Chapter 7 Coordination and Parallel Structure	Chapter 8 Connecting Ideas: 8–1, 8–2, 8–3, 8–4 Chapter 3 Future Time: 3–10	Chapter 16	Unit 8 *So, Too, Neither, Not either,* and *But*
Chapter 8 Adjective Clauses	Chapter 12 Adjective Clauses: 12–1, 12–2, 12–4, 12–5, 12–7	Chapter 13	Part VI Adjective Clauses

GRAMMAR FOR WRITING 2	FUNDAMENTALS OF ENGLISH GRAMMAR, FOURTH EDITION	UNDERSTANDING AND USING ENGLISH GRAMMAR, FOURTH EDITION	FOCUS ON GRAMMAR 4, FOURTH EDITION
Chapter 9 Adverb Clauses	Chapter 2 Past Time: 2–7 Chapter 3 Future Time: 3–6 Chapter 4 Present Perfect and Past Perfect: 4–2 Chapter 8 Connecting Ideas: 8–6, 8–7	Chapter 17: 17–1, 17–2, 17–3, 17–4, 17–5, 17–10 Chapter 19: 19–1, 19–4, 19–5, 19–6, 19–7, 19–9	–
Chapter 10 Conditionals	Chapter 3 Future Time: 3–6	Chapter 17: 17–6, 17–7, 17–8, 17–11 Chapter 20: 20–1, 20–2, 20–3, 20–4, 20–5, 20–6	Part IX Conditionals
Chapter 11 Prepositions	Chapter 6 Nouns and Pronouns: 6–4, 6–5, 6–6 Chapter 13 Gerunds and Infinitives: 13–6 Unit C: C–1, C–2		–

APPENDIX 11: ACADEMIC WORD LIST

The Academic Word List was developed in 2000 by Averil Coxhead from written material used in the fields of liberal arts, commerce, law, and science. It contains 570 words that appear most frequently in this material.

Chapter 1
accurate
adults
areas
aware
benefit
benefits
chemicals
collapsing
consequences
corporate
decades
detect
environmental
eventually
expand
factors
finally
focus
focusing
founders
ignore
incidents
license
methods
occur
occurrence
priority
prohibit
published
relaxation
relaxing
release
required
research
restrictions
role
similar
stress
survival
technological
themes
traditional
transportation
widespread

Chapter 2
access
attitude
civil
contribute
cooperation
discriminate
dramatically
environment
eventually
finally
goal
impact
impacted
involved
major
physical
physically
pursue
relying
require
responded
team
transportation

Chapter 3
affected
aspect
available
communication
computer
conventional
cultural
cultures
cycle
debate
diversity
economic
enabled
errors
files

focus
furthermore
gender
globalization
immigrants
imply
input
media
method
normally
primary
project
promote
regions
researchers
role
similar
sought
status
substitute
substituting
task
technology
text

Chapter 4
adults
affected
appreciate
areas
aspects
community
computer
conducting
consistently
consumers
create
designer
economically
gender
illegal
injure
interactive
involves

job
majority
media
occur
positive
process
relax
removed
significance
significant
similar
survey
surveyed
unique

Chapter 5
adults
author
capable
communicate
computer
conclusion
culture
cultures
dominance
factors
finance
job
motivation
period
phase
priority
process
prospects
pursue
role
sexes
signify
tasks
theme
topic
tradition
traditional

eventually
federal
goal
granted
job
major
media
methods
networking
occurs
periods
potential
primary
primarily
rely
similar
sites
source
statistics

topic
traditional
traditionally
trend
unique
vehicles

Chapter 12
academic
achieve
achieved
achieving
adult
appreciate
aspects
benefits
capabilities
capable
colleagues
communicated

communication
computer
contact
contrast
corporation
culture
decades
define
definitely
edit
errors
evaluated
eventually
factors
fees
flexible
goal
grades
job

location
negative
obviously
option
overall
policy
positive
relax
require
role
rigid
style
topic
traditional
transition
unanticipated
unattainable
unpredictable
volunteers

Appendix 1

Chapter 1
decades
economy
established
finances
financially
immigrant
job
jobs
minimum
plus
somewhat

Chapter 2
confined
detect
exhibit
exhibits
injured
injury
institute
isolate
predict
sustaining

Chapter 3
aid
assess

communication
complex
controversial
definite
display
encounter
establishing
hierarchy
identify
individuals
intelligence
intelligent
obvious
research
researcher
resident
responses
undeniable

Chapter 4
aware
commented
communities
created
cultures
diverse
diversity
equivalent
expand

feature
featured
focus
focused
highlighted
highlighting
involved
method
previous
series

Chapter 5
alternate
alternative
credits
economies
estimated
liberal
majority
options
registration
require
requirement
transfer
transferable

Chapter 6
assistant
community
consequence

decade
denied
discrimination
eventually
federal
grade
income
integral
integrate
integrated
integrating
involvement
job
jobs
legislation
predominantly
prohibited
pursue
pursuing
series
teams

Chapter 7
academia
adjustment
analyst
available
benefit
chapter

community
economics
environment
ethic
ethical
finance
goal
integrity
intelligence
logical
military
pursuing
reliance
rely
resourceful
resources
similar
stress
stressed
tasks
transition
ultimate

Chapter 8
areas
computer
conducted

demonstrate
demonstrated
designed
enhance
expand
functions
grade
instruction
issue
journal
links
manipulate
percent
proportional
published
research
researchers
series
significant
significantly
specific
transform
visualize

Chapters 9/10
area
authority

challenges
colleagues
community
consultations
consulted
design
editor
editorial
elements
energy
evaluate
evaluated
evaluates
exposed
final
implement
isolate
maintain
negative
non-traditional
philosophical
positive
practitioner
principle
sectors
vision

Chapter 11
affect
affects
attribute
chemicals
conception
cycles
definition
documented
energy
experts
focus
institute
major
percent
periods
psychology
released
researchers
respond
revealing

CREDITS

Photos

Pages 2, 25, 42, 53, 67, 68, 71, 76, 79, 93, 99, 104, 112, 120, 133, 136, 137: Shutterstock.com; **Pages 16, 20, 30, 44, 124:** iStockphoto.com; **Page 17:** Roy Garner/Alamy; **Page 28:** Image Source/Corbis; **Page 46:** CFimages/Alamy; **Page 54:** Ted Foxx/Alamy; **Page 57:** David Ball/Alamy; **Page 82:** Sinibomb Images/ Alamy; **Page 90:** Steve Hix/Somos Images/Corbis; **Page 132:** Joel W. Rogers/Corbis

Text

Pages 140–141: "Biking the distance" by Tom Ragen. Copyright © 2010. Daily Pilot. Reprinted with permission; **Pages 142–143:** Psychic Pooch by Sherry Baker. Reprinted with Permission; **Pages 144–145:** Blue Wonder by David George Gordon, a Seattle-based author. Reprinted with permission. www.davidgeorgegordon.com; **Pages 146–147:** "Latin America Film Explosion" by Frank Morales. New University Newspaper, April 10, 2000. Reprinted with permission; **Pages 148–149:** "College in China a choice" written by Tom Ragen. © 2010. Daily Pilot. Reprinted with Permission; **Pages 150–151:** "Touched by an Angel" by Janine Robinson. Orange County Woman Magazine, April 1999. Reprinted with permission; **Pages 152–153:** "Service to Country" by Laurie McLaughlin. the Indicator © 2010. Reprinted with permission; **Pages 154–155:** "Get on the Piano" by Christopher Trela. OC Family Magazine. Reprinted with Permission; **Pages 156–158:** "Feng Shui Rearranges Your Qi" by Melinda Sheckells. New University Newspaper, January 15, 2001. Reprinted with Permission; **Pages 159–161:** "Spring: Nature's way of saying let's party" by Hannah Fry. Reprinted with Permission.